The ABCs of Transformational Living

The ABCs of Transformational Living

A Journey from Attitude to Zeni-Genesis

Mike Best

Mike Best Ministries
Sunset, Texas

Copyright

Printed in the United States of America.

Publisher: Mike Best Ministries — Sunset, Texas
Cover Design & Interior: Mia Sowell

ISBN (print): 979-8-9939255-0-9
ISBN (eBook): 979-8-9939255-1-6

Dedication

To my wife, Christine Best, whose unwavering love and faith have been my steady anchor through every season. You've stood beside me through thick and thin — believing when I doubted, encouraging when I was weary, and loving me unconditionally. This journey, and every word within it, is as much yours as it is mine.

To my sons, Samuel and Justin —

Samuel, whose gracious spirit has encouraged me in my journey as a father and in my pursuit of a transformed life.

And Justin, whose fun-loving spirit and unwavering loyalty have added a richness to my life I could never have imagined.

To your wives, our grandchildren, and great-grandchildren — thank you for the joy, laughter, and strength you bring to my life. Your love reflects God's faithfulness through generations.

To my extended family and friends — your prayers and presence have been God's expressed kindness to me.

And to my church family at Grace Fellowship in Paradise, Texas — your continual encouragement, compassion, and prayers have been a living reminder of the beauty of walking in authentic community. You've shown me what grace looks like in action.

With all my heart,

Thank you.

In Loving Memory & Recognition

In Loving Memory of My Mother, Sidney Best

You taught me faith and prayer and how to walk with Jesus — day by day, step by step. Your inward strength, your open Bible, and your steady trust in God are woven into every page of this book. If faith has a fragrance, mine still carries the scent of your prayers.

In Loving Memory of My Sister, Jeanette Lincoln

We were twenty years apart and did not grow up together as kids. Yet your kindness and grace left a gentle imprint on my life. This is a brief remembrance in your honor.

With Gratitude to Mia Sowell

Thank you for bringing your gifts to this project — from the careful typesetting to the beautiful cover design. God used your creativity to shape the message and the moment this book creates in the hands of each reader.

Acknowledgments

I want to extend my heartfelt gratitude to the leadership team at Grace Fellowship in Paradise, Texas:

Chris Hurst, Rocky Johnson, Mark Morgan, and Michael Ramirez.

Each of you has been a tremendous blessing and encouragement to me throughout these past five plus years. Your vision, leadership, and love for people have created an atmosphere where faith can grow and lives can be transformed.

I'm deeply thankful for the opportunity to serve at Grace Fellowship — to play keys on the worship team, to lead a men's life group, and to co-lead a couple's life group. Your trust and support have given me a place to use my gifts for God's glory and to experience the beauty of genuine community.

Thank you for your friendship, your faith, and your steadfast example of servant leadership. You've helped me grow not just as a musician or a leader, but as a follower of Christ. I am forever grateful.

Author's Note

The image on the cover — a path leading toward a tree divided between barren ground and flourishing life — reflects much of my own story. I have walked both sides of that path. There were seasons that felt dry and demanding, and others where God's grace made things bloom in ways I never expected.

My journey was shaped early. When I was nine, my father passed away after a 22 month battle with cancer. His absence changed the rhythm of our home and required me to grow up quickly. By twelve, I was cleaning a storeroom once a week for a local appliance shop, mowing lawns in the summer, and delivering Grit Magazines to nearly a hundred homes.

My mother modeled strength, perseverance, and quiet faith through every transition. My sister — twenty years older — offered guidance from afar. And from the age of five, the piano became both a refuge and a teacher, forming discipline and devotion deep in my soul.

Years later, the Lord entrusted me with one of the greatest and most challenging gifts of my life — my daughter, Christina. From the day she was born, through twenty-eight extraordinary years, her journey taught me more about faith, surrender, perseverance, and the power of everyday miracles than any book or classroom ever could. Her life was not defined by limitation but by grace. Through her resilience, her joy, and even her suffering, I learned that transformation often unfolds slowly — through small steps, quiet prayers, and continual trust in the goodness of God.

Christina's story is woven through the margins of who I am, but this book is not about her — nor about any single season of my life. It is about the transforming work of God that meets us in every chapter of our journey: childhood responsibility, family loss, answered prayers, unanswered questions, unexpected provision, and the daily invitations to grow in character and faith.

Each letter of this book — from Attitude to Zeni-Genesis — reflects a truth God has written into my life over decades. These qualities have shaped me, corrected me, strengthened me, and continually called me to live on "the right side of the tree," where life flourishes under the warmth of His presence.

My prayer is that these pages become an invitation to transformation for you. Wherever you find yourself on the path — in barren places or in seasons of blessing — may you discover the God who walks with you, shapes you, and invites you into a life renewed from the inside out.

— Mike Best

The Journey of Becoming

Every lasting change begins with a single, sacred choice — to allow God to renew the way you think, see, and live. Transformation doesn't arrive in a sudden flash; it unfolds one thought, one attitude, one surrendered moment at a time.

This book is a roadmap of twenty-six qualities that shape how we think, live, and love. Each letter of the alphabet — from Attitude to Zeni-Genesis — reveals a spiritual truth designed to deepen your walk with Christ. These are not abstract ideas or motivational phrases. They are living principles, rooted in Scripture and proven in the ordinary and extraordinary moments of life.

If you could see the cover of this book as a picture of the heart, you would see two sides of a single path — one barren and dry, the other flourishing with life. That path leading toward the tree is a picture of the choices we make every day. We can live on the left — weary, striving, spiritually dry — or we can live on the right, where growth, renewal, and abundance take root.

This book is an invitation to step onto the right side of the path — an invitation to transformation.

I call it the journey of becoming, because that's what following Jesus truly is. Becoming the person God created you to be isn't about self-help, self-effort, or self-improvement. It is a Spirit-led transformation — the slow, sacred work of aligning your thoughts, desires, and decisions with the heart of God until your inner world reflects His truth.

So, bring your hopes, your hurts, your questions, and even your quiet longings. God delights in meeting you exactly where you are. He specializes in turning barren ground into gardens of grace. If you've been waiting for a fresh start, a clearer path, or a deeper walk with Him, let these pages become your open door.

Transformation happens letter by letter, layer by layer.

You may begin with Attitude, seeing life through God's perspective.

Then move to Behavior, where conviction becomes action.

As you continue, each quality builds upon the last, forming a life anchored in faith, saturated in gratitude, and strengthened by grace.

And when you arrive at Zeni-Genesis, you discover the miracle of new birth — the new beginning Jesus offers to every surrendered heart. It is the starting point of God's transformative work, where He initiates a renewed life and sets your steps on an upward, rising path toward Him.

Throughout this journey, you will find stories, Scriptures, and reflections inviting you to pause. These are not interruptions to the reading — they are sacred spaces where transformation takes root. Slow down. Let each principle breathe. Listen for the Spirit's whisper between the lines. The goal is not to rush through the alphabet; the goal is to become more like Jesus with every step.

The promise of Philippians 1:6 is your steady companion:

> *"And I am certain that God, who began the good work within you, will continue His work until it is finally finished on the day when Christ Jesus returns."*

So, let's begin — with Attitude, the inner posture of the heart that shapes the direction of your life and becomes the first step toward living on the flourishing side of the path."

How to Use This Book

The ABCs of Transformational Living is not meant to be rushed. It is designed to be walked through — prayerfully, personally, and at your own pace.

Each letter represents a spiritual quality that God uses to shape a transformed life. While the book follows the alphabet from Attitude to Zeni-Genesis, transformation doesn't always happen in order. You are free to linger, revisit, or pause wherever the Spirit leads.

Suggested Reading Approaches

1. **Daily Devotional Journey** — Consider reading one chapter per day. Allow the Scripture, story, and Reflect & Apply questions to guide your prayer and journaling time.

2. **Weekly Reflection Rhythm** — Read one letter per week. Return to the chapter multiple times, practicing the principle throughout the week before moving on.

3. **Small Group or Life Group Study** — Read the chapter individually, then discuss the Reflect & Apply questions together. Let shared stories and Scripture deepen the transformation God is doing in each life.

4. **Spirit-Led Reading** — If a particular letter resonates with your current season — begin there. God often meets us where our need is greatest.

How to Engage the Pages

Pause often. Transformation happens in reflection, not speed.

Journal freely. Write prayers, questions, and insights in the margins or a separate notebook.

Pray honestly. Each chapter closes with a prayer — make it your own.

Practice faithfully. These principles take root through daily obedience, not perfection.

This book is not about completing the alphabet.

It is about becoming more like Christ — trusting the God who is faithfully at work in you, one surrendered step at a time.

Contents

Part I — Foundations of Inner Renewal (A–G)

Part II — Formation of Character (H–N)

Part III — Faith in Action (O–U)

Part IV — Fulfillment of Transformation (V–Z)

Contents

Conclusion

ATTITUDE

THE POWER OF PERSPECTIVE

The roar of the engine filled my ears as the small Cessna 150 trembled against the crosswind. My hands gripped the yoke tightly, knuckles white, as my instructor's voice crackled through the headset: "Easy pressure — don't fight the air. Just adjust your attitude."

That day, at sixteen years old, I wasn't just learning how to fly a plane — I was learning one of the most valuable lessons of my life. The word "attitude," in aviation, doesn't refer to mood; it describes the airplane's orientation relative to the horizon. Pull back slightly, and the nose lift — the plane climbs. Push forward too far, and you descend. The smallest movement can determine whether you rise, stall, or soar.

As I leveled out and the horizon steadied in front of me, the instructor's words took root deeper than he realized: "Your attitude determines your altitude." Years later, I've learned that the same truth governs our spiritual lives. Our attitude — the lens through which we see God, others, and ourselves — determines how high or low our spirit flies.

"Let this mind be in you which was also in Christ Jesus."
~ Philippians 2:5 (NLT)

When Paul wrote these words to the Philippians, he was sitting in a prison cell, yet his heart overflowed with gratitude and peace. He had learned that joy wasn't dependent on circumstance — it flowed from perspective. While the world says, "Change your situation to be happy," Scripture teaches, "Change your perspective and you'll see God's hand in your situation."

Attitude is the cockpit of the soul. It controls our spiritual direction long before our external conditions change. I've met people who, despite hardship, radiate peace and hope. Their secret isn't denial — it's divine focus. They've learned to adjust their spiritual instruments when life's turbulence hits.

Maybe you've been there — when life's winds push against you, and you feel like you're losing altitude. A doctor's report, a financial setback, a strained relationship — moments that make you want to pull the throttle and quit. But just as in that cockpit years ago, the Spirit of God leans close and whispers: *"Adjust your attitude."*

"Fix your thoughts on what is true, and honorable, and right, and pure, and lovely, and admirable. Think about things that are excellent and worthy of praise."
~ Philippians 4:8 (NLT)

The challenge is that our natural instinct is to focus on what's wrong — on the storm clouds instead of the sunlight beyond them. But when we fix our thoughts on truth instead of turmoil, our heart begins to steady. Gratitude, humility, and trust become the instruments that help us climb above the chaos.

One of the most freeing realizations in my life was understanding that I can't always control what happens to me, but I can control how I respond to it. **Attitude isn't pretending everything's perfect; it's choosing faith even when it isn't.** It's saying, *"God, I can't change this situation, but I trust You're still in control of the sky around me."*

There have been seasons when I faced storms I never saw coming — losses that left me gasping for air. And yet, through every dark cloud, I learned something sacred: perspective doesn't come from comfort; it comes from surrender. When we give God permission to shape our thoughts, He recalibrates our hearts to see what He's doing even in the unseen.

Attitude is what keeps worship alive in the waiting. It's what makes a person sing through sorrow or find purpose in pain. I've watched people walk through grief with peace that defies logic — and every time, I think of that small Cessna climbing against the wind.

It's not that the air stops resisting — it's that the pilot learns how to rise *because* of it.

Principles for the Journey

Every flight of faith begins in the mind. Before we can live transformed, we must learn to think transformed.

1. ATTITUDE SHAPES PEACE

Peace doesn't come from the absence of storms but from the presence of Christ within them.

"You will keep in perfect peace all who trust in you, all whose thoughts are fixed on you!"
~ Isaiah 26:3 (NLT)

When our focus shifts from fear to faith, anxiety loses its grip. Perspective doesn't erase problems — it magnifies God's power above them.

2. ATTITUDE FUELS ALTITUDE THROUGH GRATITUDE

A thankful heart lifts the soul higher than complaint ever could.

"Be thankful in all circumstances, for this is God's will for you who belong to Christ Jesus."
~ 1 Thessalonians 5:18 (NLT)

Gratitude changes the air we breathe. It teaches us to look for grace in the ordinary and hope in the hard places.

3. ATTITUDE IS STEADIED BY HUMILITY

A prideful heart loses balance quickly, but humility anchors us.

> *"Don't be selfish; don't try to impress others. Be humble, thinking of others as better than yourselves."*
> *~ Philippians 2:3 (NLT)*

The lower we bow, the higher God lifts us. A humble attitude creates lift where arrogance creates drag.

4. ATTITUDE CORRECTS OUR COURSE THROUGH FAITH

When fear clouds the horizon, faith becomes our compass.

> *"For we live by believing and not by seeing."*
> *~ 2 Corinthians 5:7 (NLT)*

Faith doesn't ignore reality — it redefines it. It reminds us that God is still sovereign, even when the instruments flicker and visibility fades.

5. ATTITUDE KEEPS HOPE ON THE HORIZON

Every believer needs a forward focus. Hope points the way when we can't yet see the destination.

> *"This hope is a strong and trustworthy anchor*
> *for our souls."*
> *~ Hebrews 6:19 (NLT)*

When we lift our eyes toward the horizon of eternity, present troubles lose their power to define us. Hope steadies our climb.

Reflect & Apply

1. What current situation in your life feels like turbulence, and how might a shift in attitude change your response?

2. When have you experienced peace even though your circumstances didn't change?

3. How can gratitude transform your daily outlook this week?

4. What "altitude" do you sense God calling you to rise to — spiritually, relationally, or emotionally?

5. Where might God be inviting you to surrender control and trust His direction again?

Lord, teach me to adjust my attitude when life feels turbulent. Help me fix my thoughts on You instead of my fears. When the horizon disappears, remind me that You are still my pilot, still in control. Lift my perspective so I can see Your purpose, even through the clouds. Give me a grateful heart, a humble spirit, and a faith that flies above the storm. Amen.

BEHAVIOR

WALKING WHAT WE BELIEVE

The meeting room was quiet except for the hum of the projector. Numbers filled the screen — one line stood out like a red warning light. We'd made an expensive mistake. I felt the weight of every eye in the room. I could smooth it over, adjust a formula, and no one would ever know. Or I could take responsibility.

In that pause, a verse echoed through my mind:

> *"You can identify them by their actions."*
> *~ Matthew 7:16 (NLT)*

I swallowed hard. "That one's on me," I said aloud. A few heads lifted, surprised. The moment passed, the meeting ended — and yet, something in the atmosphere shifted. Instead of criticism, there was trust. My team began owning their own missteps, helping one another correct them. That day taught me a truth no leadership manual could capture: **integrity is contagious**.

> *"Let this mind be in you which was also in Christ Jesus."*
> *~ Philippians 2:5 (NLT)*

Behavior is belief in motion. It's the visible rhythm of the heart. Anyone can talk about faith; only our actions prove what we truly trust.

> *"Those who say they live in God should live their lives as Jesus did."*
> *~ 1 John 2:6 (NLT)*

The longer I follow Jesus, the more I see that transformation isn't about learning new information; it's about living new patterns — choosing Christlike responses where my old habits used to rule. The world doesn't need louder Christians — it needs truer ones. People are starving for authenticity, for someone whose private life matches their public worship.

I remember an afternoon in the grocery store. The cashier was flustered, her hands shaking as she fumbled with the register. I was in a hurry, frustrated, ready to let impatience leak out. Then a gentle nudge in my spirit whispered, "Grace looks like patience." I took a breath, smiled, and told her to take her time.

Weeks later, I saw her again. She looked up and said, "You're the guy who didn't get mad." That small act — a moment of self-control — became a sermon louder than words.

Behavior isn't just obedience; it's worship. Each decision to act with grace is a quiet "hallelujah." Each moment we choose kindness over pride, mercy over convenience, we reflect the One who loved first.

> *"Whatever you do or say, do it as a representative of the Lord Jesus, giving thanks through him to God the Father."*
> *~ Colossians 3:17 (NLT)*

We represent Him — everywhere. At home, in traffic, in the break room, online. Our tone becomes our testimony. Our patience becomes our pulpit. Even when no one else sees, heaven watches, and God smiles.

But sometimes we stumble. Behavior falters. Words come out sharper than intended; frustration spills where grace should've poured. Failure can make us feel disqualified, yet that's where grace begins its best work. The same repentance that kneels low lifts us higher than before. A humble apology can preach the gospel more powerfully than flawless performance.

I once watched a coworker defend someone who wasn't in the room. Others were criticizing him; she quietly said, "He's not here to speak for himself — let's stop." The conversation froze. She didn't quote Scripture, but she lived it. Her courage rebuked gossip and modeled respect. That's the power of behavior filled with light — it changes the environment without needing to explain itself.

Principles for the Journey

Every day preaches something. The only question is — what sermon are we living?

1. BEHAVIOR REVEALS BELIEF

Our actions are windows to our faith.

"For the mouth speaks what the heart is full of."
~ Luke 6:45 (NLT)

When the heart is anchored in God's goodness, peace and honesty flow naturally. When it's anchored in fear, control takes over.

2. BEHAVIOR EXPRESSES LOVE THROUGH OBEDIENCE

Love becomes visible the moment obedience steps into the room.

"If you love me, obey my commandments."
~ John 14:15 (NLT)

Love and obedience aren't rivals; they're reflections. Every "yes" to God is an act of devotion, not duty. When love leads, obedience follows.

3. BEHAVIOR GAINS CREDIBILITY THROUGH CONSISTENCY

Character is not proven in big moments but in the quiet repetition of choosing what's right.

"Let's not merely say that we love each other; let us show the truth by our actions."
~ 1 John 3:18 (NLT)

Consistency is the heartbeat of integrity. People may forget our words, but they never forget how we live. And when we fail, honesty rebuilds what hypocrisy destroys. A simple, "I was wrong, please forgive me," repairs more than silence ever could.

4. BEHAVIOR BEARS FRUIT WHEN TRANSFORMATION IS REAL

The truest evidence of change isn't what we claim — it's what we naturally produce.

"The Holy Spirit produces this kind of fruit in our lives: love, joy, peace, patience, kindness, goodness, faithfulness, gentleness, and self-control."
~ Galatians 5:22-23 (NLT)

Behavior isn't self-improvement — it's Spirit-empowerment. As we stay connected to the Vine, fruit grows naturally.

5. BEHAVIOR WALKS BY FAITH WHEN SIGHT IS UNCLEAR

Faith is never louder than when our feet move before the path becomes clear.

"For we live by believing and not by seeing."
~ 2 Corinthians 5:7 (NLT)

When sight is dim, our behavior reveals what we truly believe — acting on God's Word even when clarity hasn't come.

6. BEHAVIOR IS THE BRIDGE BETWEEN HEARING AND DOING

Faith becomes real the moment we step from hearing into doing.

"But don't just listen to God's word. You must do what it says."
~ James 1:22 (NLT)

Truth doesn't transform until it's lived. Every time belief becomes behavior, heaven touches earth through us.

Reflect & Apply

1. Think about a recent moment when your reaction revealed what you truly believed. What did it show you about your heart?

2. Where do you struggle most to live out what you believe — home, work, or in quiet moments?

3. When you fall short, how can humility and repentance rebuild trust in your relationships?

4. What fruit of the Spirit is God currently developing in you, and how does it show through your actions?

5. How might your consistent behavior this week become a silent testimony to someone watching?

Father, let my life echo what I profess. When I'm tempted to react in frustration, remind me that grace can change the atmosphere. Teach me to obey with love, to act with courage, to live with integrity. May my everyday behavior become an act of worship that points others to You. Amen.

COMMITMENT

TURNING INTENTIONS INTO RESULTS

It was one of those long Texas summer days where the air feels heavy and the sun seems to hang motionless in the sky. I'd been working on a project that had stretched me to the edge of exhaustion. Every part of me wanted to quit — to walk away and start fresh later. But something inside whispered, *"Don't stop now. You're closer than you think."*

That's the thing about commitment. It doesn't make life easy; it makes it meaningful.

Every worthwhile thing God builds in our lives requires endurance. Dreams fade without discipline. Passion fades without persistence. Commitment is the bridge between good intentions and lasting fruit.

I think of the farmer who wakes before dawn, day after day, tending soil that hasn't yet produced a single sprout. His back aches, his hands are cracked, but he still goes out to the field because he believes harvest is coming. He doesn't quit just because he can't see results. Faithful commitment looks foolish at first — until the rain comes.

> *"So let's not get tired of doing what is good. At just the right time we will reap a harvest of blessing if we don't give up."*
> *~ Galatians 6:9 (NLT)*

Commitment is tested not in the beginning but in the middle — the long, ordinary stretch between promise and fulfillment. That's where the voices of doubt get loudest, and the temptation to give up feels strongest. But it's also where roots grow deep. The soil of waiting strengthens what the surface of success can't.

When I look back on my own life, I can trace God's faithfulness through the seasons I wanted to quit but didn't. Years ago, when I lost my job after 9/11, it felt like the bottom dropped out from under me. It was three long years before full-time work came again. I worked multiple jobs, piecing together enough to keep our family afloat. Some days it was all I could do to keep believing that something better was ahead. Yet in that wilderness, God was shaping endurance. He was teaching me that commitment to His call doesn't depend on convenience — it depends on trust.

I learned that when you can't see what God is doing, commitment means showing up anyway. Keep plowing. Keep praying. Keep praising. You might not see growth yet, but heaven's already counting the harvest.

> *"The testing of your faith produces perseverance. Let perseverance finish its work so that you may be mature and complete, not lacking anything."*
> *~ James 1:3–4 (NLT)*

Faith matures in the tension between "not yet" and "still believing." That's where character forms. Commitment isn't glamorous — It's often quiet, unseen, and uncelebrated. But it's sacred work. God does His deepest shaping in hidden seasons.

When Jesus set His face toward the cross, He modeled ultimate commitment. Every step was deliberate. Every prayer was surrendered. He didn't quit when it hurt. He didn't turn back when the crowd grew silent. Love held Him steady. That's what real commitment looks like — obedience that outlasts emotion.

Principles for the Journey

Commitment is the quiet fire that keeps you moving forward long after the feeling fades.

1. COMMITMENT ANCHORS GROWTH

True growth doesn't happen in bursts of inspiration but through steady obedience.

"If you are faithful in little things, you will be faithful in large ones."
~ Luke 16:10 (NLT)

Every small "yes" strengthens your spiritual muscle. The more you keep showing up, the more capacity God gives you to endure.

2. COMMITMENT TURNS PERSEVERANCE INTO PURPOSE

When commitment feels costly, the Word reminds us that God has already marked out the race and given us strength to finish it.

"Let us run with endurance the race God has set before us."
~ Hebrews 12:1 (NLT)

Endurance is what turns calling into completion. Without it, even the strongest start won't last. Commitment keeps purpose from unraveling when progress feels slow.

3. COMMITMENT IN OBSCURITY PREPARES YOU FOR OPPORTUNITY

David learned faithfulness tending sheep long before he faced Goliath.

"Then Samuel said to Jesse, 'Send for him at once.' ... So as David stood there among his brothers, Samuel took the flask of olive oil he had brought and anointed David."
~ 1 Samuel 16:11–13 (NLT)

The hidden seasons are where God anoints hearts before He appoints platforms.

4. COMMITMENT TURNS TRIALS INTO TRAINING

Every obstacle becomes an opportunity for spiritual conditioning.

"We can rejoice, too, when we run into problems and trials, for we know that they help us develop endurance."
~ Romans 5:3 (NLT)

Each challenge, delay, or disappointment is sharpening your faith for greater responsibility.

5. COMMITMENT IS SUSTAINED BY LOVE

At the core of every lasting commitment is love — not obligation.

"Three things will last forever — faith, hope, and love — and the greatest of these is love."
~ 1 Corinthians 13:13 (NLT)

Love is the fuel that keeps obedience burning long after emotion fades. It transforms endurance from drudgery into devotion.

Reflect & Apply

1. Where in your life are you tempted to give up too soon?

2. What "middle season" are you currently in — and what might God be growing in you through it?

3. How can you strengthen your commitment to what God's asked of you this week?

4. Who in your life models steadfast commitment, and what can you learn from their example?

5. What is one specific commitment you will follow through on this week, and what will help you stay consistent?

Prayer

Father, strengthen my heart to walk in steady, faithful commitment. When the middle feels long and my motivation fades, remind me that You are shaping endurance within me. Teach me to show up with a willing spirit, even on the days when progress seems slow or hidden. Help me choose obedience over emotion, devotion over distraction, and perseverance over quitting. May every small "yes" become an offering of love to You. Anchor my steps, steady my resolve, and align my heart with Your purposes — so I can finish the work You've entrusted to me with grace and integrity. Amen.

DISCIPLINE

TRAINING THE HEART FOR HOLINESS

The early morning air was cool, the kind that carries both silence and promise. I sat in my car outside the gym, staring at the door like it was a mountain. The battle wasn't against the treadmill — it was against my own resistance. Every part of me whispered, *"You can skip just this once."*

I smiled, because I knew that voice well. It wasn't just about exercise — it was about discipline, about doing what's right even when comfort argues louder. That morning, as I finally pushed open the door, another truth stirred in my heart: the hardest part of discipline is almost always the decision to begin.

Spiritual growth works much the same way. We want strength without struggle, wisdom without repetition, holiness without surrender. But God's pattern has always been to shape us through steady, daily obedience — the small "yeses" that become habits of holiness.

"God's discipline is always good for us, so that we might share in his holiness."
~ Hebrews 12:10 (NLT)

Discipline isn't punishment; it's preparation. God's correction isn't rooted in condemnation but in love. He never disciplines to break us down — only to build us up, to shape our desires so they align with His. Like a craftsman sanding rough wood, His work may feel abrasive in the moment, but every stroke smooths the surface until it can reflect His image.

There was a season when God's discipline showed up in my life not as correction, but as delay. I had prayed for breakthrough, for open doors, for opportunities that seemed right. Instead, the doors stayed shut. I didn't realize then that God was training my patience muscle. He wasn't denying me — He was developing me. The waiting became my classroom, and the lesson was trust.

Discipline teaches us to keep walking even when the path feels slow. It turns duty into devotion. Every time we choose prayer over distraction, forgiveness over bitterness, integrity over impulse, we train our souls in holiness. And over time, that training produces something beautiful — freedom.

"No discipline is enjoyable while it is happening — it's painful! But afterward there will be a peaceful harvest of right living for those who are trained in this way."
~ Hebrews 12:11 (NLT)

Holiness grows in the hidden rhythms of consistency. The same way a musician practices scales or an athlete trains muscles, the believer exercises faith through obedience. We don't drift into maturity; we discipline our way there by grace.

I remember Mrs. Ellis, my piano teacher from childhood. Week after week, she'd make me practice finger drills and scales. I didn't understand why then — I just wanted to play songs. But she knew that repetition builds readiness. The strength in my fingers was forming long before the music flowed from them.

Years later, I realized God works the same way. The repetition of spiritual disciplines — prayer, study, worship, generosity — forms spiritual muscle memory. You may not notice the growth day to day, but one day, your reflex becomes faith instead of fear, praise instead of panic.

Discipline doesn't enslave you — it equips you. It prepares you for moments when you'll need spiritual strength without hesitation. It trains your heart to respond like Jesus, not react like the flesh.

Principles for the Journey

Discipline is where God shapes the soul — one choice, one correction, one surrendered moment at a time.

1. DISCIPLINE LEADS TO FREEDOM

God's correction doesn't restrict us; it releases us into true strength.

"Then Jesus said to the people who believed in him,
'You are truly my disciples if you remain faithful to my teachings. And you will know the truth, and the truth will set you free."
~ John 8:31-32 (NLT)

Freedom isn't doing whatever we want; it's the ability to do what's right without being ruled by what's wrong.

2. DISCIPLINE GROWS THROUGH REPETITION

Faith grows in the mundane before it shows up in the miraculous.

"Practice these things; immerse yourself in them, so that all may see your progress."
~ 1 Timothy 4:15 (NLT)

Every small act of obedience prepares you for greater responsibility.

3. DISCIPLINE SHOWS THE FATHER'S CARE

God's discipline is evidence of His love, not His anger.

"For the Lord disciplines those he loves ..."
~ Hebrews 12:6 (NLT)

The Father trains those He treasures. His correction isn't meant to harm us but to prepare us — shaping our character, strengthening our faith, and proving that we truly belong to Him.

4. DISCIPLINE STRENGTHENS PERSEVERANCE

When God allows challenges into our path, He is building spiritual stamina that can withstand the weight of real life.

"We can rejoice, too, when we run into problems and trials, for we know that they help us develop endurance. And endurance develops strength of character, and character strengthens our confident hope of salvation."
~ Romans 5:3-4 (NLT)

Peace is the harvest of those who continue walking with God even when the lesson is hard. Discipline shapes endurance, and endurance forms resilience.

5. DISCIPLINE FORMS HABITS THAT LEAD TO HOLINESS

Every repeated act of obedience becomes a stepping stone toward a life that reflects Christ more clearly.

"Train yourself to be godly. Physical training is good, but training for godliness is much better, promising benefits in this life and in the life to come."
~ 1 Timothy 4:7-8 (NLT)

Discipline doesn't just improve us — it transforms us. Holy habits become the melody of a heart trained by grace.

Reflect & Apply

1. How do you usually respond when God's discipline feels uncomfortable?

____
____
____
____
____
____
____
____

2. What area of your life might God be training right now through repetition or waiting?

____
____
____
____
____
____
____
____

3. How can spiritual discipline become an act of love rather than obligation?

4. What daily practice could help you strengthen your "faith muscle" this week?

5. In what ways has God's correction ultimately brought peace or maturity to your life?

Prayer

Father, thank You for loving me enough to train me. Teach me to see Your discipline not as punishment but as preparation. Help me stay faithful in the routines that shape my character. When I resist correction, remind me that You're forming something eternal in me. Give me the endurance to finish every lesson and the grace to reflect Your holiness. Amen.

ENCOURAGEMENT

FUEL FOR ENDURANCE

It was noon when I pulled into Midland, Texas. The long drive had given me time to pray, but not to prepare. I was going to visit my nephew — young, brave, and walking a hard road through cancer.

When I arrived, he greeted me with that same calm, steady smile I'd always known. We sat together for a while — just me and him, exchanging quiet conversation and the kind of stillness that feels holy. We talked about Scripture, about heaven, about God's goodness in the middle of mystery. The peace in his eyes said more than either of us could.

As the evening shadows stretched across the yard, I stood to leave. He looked up and said softly, *"Thank you for coming. I felt God's presence and peace while we were talking."*

Driving away that evening, tears welled in my eyes. I realized something that sank deep into my spirit — **encouragement isn't about having the right words; it's about carrying the right presence**. Sometimes, the most powerful encouragement doesn't sound like a sermon; it looks like showing up.

> *"So encourage each other and build each other up, just as you are already doing."*
> *~ 1 Thessalonians 5:11 (NLT)*

Encouragement is sacred oxygen for weary souls. It doesn't erase hardship — it gives strength to breathe through it. The word encourage literally means to come alongside, to lend courage to someone who feels their own slipping away.

There have been times in my life when a simple act of kindness carried me farther than the giver could have known. After my daughter Christina passed, encouragement came in quiet forms — cards, meals, gentle words whispered in prayer. Each one was a lifeline reminding me: you're not alone.

Encouragement is heaven's way of speaking through human voices. It doesn't always fix pain, but it always brings light into it. And often, the people who encourage us the most are walking through their own storms yet still choose to lift others higher.

> *"Anxiety weighs down the heart, but a kind word cheers it up."*
> *~ Proverbs 12:25 (NLT)*

A kind word. A thoughtful text. A visit made in faith. These small moments are how the kingdom advances — one heart strengthened at a time. You may never see the full impact of your encouragement, but God multiplies every seed you plant.

In Acts 4, a man named Joseph was nicknamed Barnabas — "son of encouragement." He wasn't known for wealth or titles, but for lifting others. When the church doubted Paul's conversion, Barnabas believed in him When John Mark failed and others turned away, Barnabas gave him another chance. That single act of grace eventually helped birth the Gospel of Mark. Encouragement changes destinies. It is the language of grace in motion.

Principles for the Journey

Encouragement is the breath of God passed from one heart to another, awakening strength where weakness once lived.

1. ENCOURAGEMENT STRENGTHENS WEARY HEARTS

Even the smallest gesture can renew hope.

"The Sovereign Lord has given me his words of wisdom, so that I know how to comfort the weary."
~ Isaiah 50:4 (NLT)

Your presence may be the sermon someone's soul needs to hear.

2. ENCOURAGEMENT REFLECTS THE HEART OF GOD

When we lift others, we echo His compassion.

He is the God of all comfort. He comforts us in all our troubles so that we can comfort others.
~ 2 Corinthians 1:3-4 (NLT)

Every word of comfort is a reflection of His unfailing love.

3. ENCOURAGEMENT MULTIPLIES COURAGE

Barnabas lifted Paul; Paul lifted Timothy; Timothy lifted the Church.

"Let us think of ways to motivate one another to acts of love and good works."
~ Hebrews 10:24 (NLT)

Every word of comfort is a reflection of His unfailing love.

4. ENCOURAGEMENT IS AN ACT OF WORSHIP

When we refresh others, we refresh the heart of Christ Himself.

"The generous will prosper; those who refresh others will themselves be refreshed."
~ Proverbs 11:25 (NLT)

To lift another's burden is to join Jesus in His ministry of compassion.

5. ENCOURAGEMENT IS A DISCIPLINE OF THE HEART

It takes practice to speak hope even when life feels heavy.

"Kind words are like honey — sweet to the soul and healthy for the body."
~ Proverbs 16:24 (NLT)

The more we train our hearts to look for God's goodness, the more naturally our words will lift the weary around us.

Reflect & Apply

1. Who in your life is walking through a difficult season and could use your presence or encouragement today?

2. Think of a time someone encouraged you unexpectedly. How did it strengthen your faith?

3. How can you intentionally build encouragement into your daily habits?

4. What would it look like to become a modern-day "Barnabas" in your family, workplace, or church?

5. What simple act — call, card, or visit — might God be prompting you to do this week?

Father, thank You for the steady gift of encouragement. Thank You for the people who showed up when I needed hope, and for letting me be that presence to others. Teach me to listen deeply, to speak gently, and to notice the ones who are running low on courage. Let my words carry peace, and my presence carry You. In every conversation, let others feel Your nearness. Amen.

FAITH

BELIEVING BEFORE SEEING

The light in our kitchen was dim that evening, the kind of amber glow that made the whole room feel smaller. I was nine years old, sitting at the table with my mother. The table was set — two plates, two forks, and two glasses — but there wasn't any food.

The house was quiet except for the faint hum of the refrigerator and the slow ticking of the wall clock. My father had passed away from cancer not long before, and Mom was doing her best to hold life together. She had taken a job as a Health Unit Coordinator at Midland Memorial Hospital, working double shifts just to make ends meet. But that week, there wasn't anything left. Payday was still a few days away.

Still, she set the table. She didn't pace the floor or call someone to complain. She just laid out the plates like she always did, then sat down, folded her hands, and bowed her head.

Her voice was calm, steady — almost tender.

"Father," she prayed, "thank You that Your promises are true. You said in Your Word that You will never leave us nor forsake us. You have promised that the righteous are never forsaken, nor their children left begging for bread. And You have assured us that You will supply all our needs according to Your riches in glory. So, Lord, we thank You in advance for Your provision."

I sat there with one eye open, glancing at my empty plate, half expecting food to just appear. We waited for a few moments — long enough for a little boy to start wondering how faith worked. Then, the phone rang.

Mom got up and answered. It was a lady from our church. "You've been on my mind all day," she said. "I felt like the Lord wanted me to bring you some food."

When she arrived, her car was full — bags of groceries, more than enough to last until Mom got paid. I remember watching her carry those sacks inside, the sound of paper rustling and cans clinking, and realizing something that's never left me: **Faith doesn't deny what's empty; it believes God can fill it.**

That night, my mother's faith became my first real picture of God's provision. She didn't panic, and she didn't plead. She just believed.

> *"Faith shows the reality of what we hope for; it is the evidence of things we cannot see."*
> *~ Hebrews 11:1 (NLT)*

Faith isn't pretending everything is fine; it's trusting that God is still faithful when nothing seems to be. It's the quiet conviction that His promise outweighs our problem.

FAITH IN THE EMPTY JAR

There's a story in Scripture that echoes my mother's prayer.

In *1 Kings 17*, a widow in Zarephath was preparing her last meal. The drought had stolen everything — her flour was almost gone, her oil nearly dry. When the prophet Elijah asked for bread, she told him, "I only have a handful of flour left in the jar and a little cooking oil in the jug."

> **Elijah answered with faith that saw beyond the jar:**
> *"Don't be afraid! Go ahead and do just what you've said, but make a little bread for me first. Then use what's left to prepare a meal for yourself and your son. For this is what the Lord, the God of Israel, says: There will always be flour and olive oil left in your containers until the time when the Lord sends rain."*
> *~ 1 Kings 17:13-14 (NLT)*

The widow believed — and she baked.

Every morning after that, she reached into the same jar and found enough. It wasn't overflowing; it was sufficient. Faith doesn't always fill the pantry overnight. Sometimes it just keeps the jar from running dry.

My mom's prayer taught me that truth in a different way. God's provision may come suddenly or steadily, but faith rests in the confidence that He will provide — however He chooses to do it.

Principles for the Journey

Faith is the courage to step into the unknown because you trust the One who stands in it.

1. Faith Looks Beyond What's Missing to What God Has Promised

Before we see anything change on the outside, faith begins its work on the inside — shifting our eyes from what is lacking to the God who never lacks anything.

"For we live by believing and not by seeing."
~ 2 Corinthians 5:7 (NLT)

Faith doesn't wait for evidence before it acts. It moves forward based on who God is, not what we see.

2. Faith Grows Strongest in Scarcity

It is often in our emptiest seasons that God teaches us His deepest truths. When our resources run out, His strength steps in.

"My grace is all you need. My power works best in weakness."
~ 2 Corinthians 12:9 (NLT)

When we have nothing left to rely on, we discover that God is everything we need.

3. FAITH THANKS GOD BEFORE THE MIRACLE

Gratitude is faith's first language. When we thank God in advance, we declare that His promise is more real to us than our present need.

"With thanksgiving, present your requests to God."
~ Philippians 4:6 (NLT)

My mother's prayer began with gratitude before provision appeared. Gratitude waters the seeds of faith.

4. FAITH INSPIRES FAITH IN OTHERS

The faith we live out becomes a testimony someone else stands on. When we hold steady, we show the world what trust in God looks like.

"Let us hold tightly without wavering to the hope we affirm, for God can be trusted to keep His promise."
~ Hebrews 10:23 (NLT)

Faith is contagious. My mother's simple act of trust that day planted a lifelong belief in me that God truly provides.

5. **FAITH DOESN'T DEMAND CLARITY — IT CHOOSES CONFIDENCE**

We don't need to understand the path when we trust the One who leads us. Faith rests in the certainty of His character, not the clarity of our circumstances.

"Trust in the Lord with all your heart; do not depend on your own understanding."
~ Proverbs 3:5 (NLT)

You don't need to know how God will do it; you just need to believe that He will.

Reflect & Apply

1. When was the last time you had to believe God for something you couldn't see yet?

2. How has God provided for you in unexpected ways, even when the situation seemed hopeless?

3. What promise from God are you holding onto right now? How can you show faith in action this week?

4. Think of someone whose faith encouraged you when you were struggling. How can you pass that encouragement forward?

5. Where in your life do you need to move from waiting to trusting?

Heavenly Father, thank You for being faithful even when I can't see the outcome. When life feels empty, teach me to trust that You are already working behind the scenes. Give me a heart that believes Your promises more than my circumstances. Help me thank You before I see the answer, and worship You while I wait. May my faith inspire others to believe that You are who You say You are. Amen.

GRATITUDE

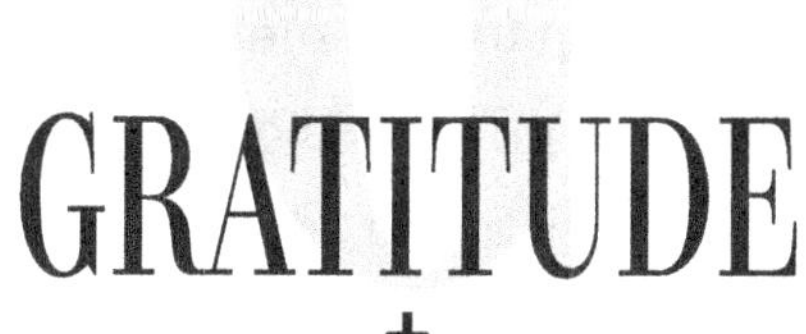

SHIFTING OUR GAZE FROM WHAT'S MISSING TO WHAT'S PRESENT

Faith teaches us to trust before we see. Gratitude teaches us to thank before we feel. One reaches forward in hope; the other looks upward in worship. Together, they create the rhythm of a transformed heart.

The Note That Changed My Morning

The day after Christina passed away, our house was full of people — family, friends, casseroles, and compassion. Love was everywhere, but grief pressed down like a heavy blanket. I remember sitting in my living room feeling like I couldn't breathe. I loved everyone who was there, but I needed space ... space to think, to grieve, to find God in the middle of it all.

So, I grabbed my keys and drove to Starbucks. I stood in line, half there and half somewhere else. I wasn't looking for gratitude that morning — honestly, I didn't have the strength for it. But sometimes God plants the seeds of gratitude in places we don't expect, long before we have the capacity to recognize them.

A good friend called to check on me, and as I answered, I could hear my own voice crack beneath the weight of loss. "I'm okay," I said, though I wasn't. When I reached the counter, the barista smiled softly and slid a cup toward me.

"It's already taken care of," she said.

There was a Post-it stuck to the lid. In neat handwriting were three simple words: **God sees you!**

I just stared at it. Something in me broke — but not in a destructive way. It was the kind of breaking that releases ... the kind that makes room for healing. In that moment, gratitude didn't arrive as a feeling; it arrived as a reminder. God had slipped a small, quiet kindness into the middle of my pain, and gratitude began to flicker like the first light of morning.

I wasn't grateful for the loss — but I was grateful for the God who refused to let me walk through that loss unseen.

That Post-it note didn't erase grief, but it shifted my gaze. Gratitude does that — it redirects your vision from what has been taken to what God has placed right in front of you. And Scripture calls us not just to feel gratitude but to choose it, right where we stand.

> *"Be thankful in all circumstances, for this is God's will for you who belong to Christ Jesus."*
> *~ 1 Thessalonians 5:18 (NLT)*

Gratitude doesn't deny the difficulty; it declares that God is still good in the middle of it. It doesn't wait for everything to feel right — it chooses to see what is right.

The Practice That Shifts the Soul

Gratitude is one of the most powerful spiritual disciplines we can develop. It's not a personality trait or a mood — it's a deliberate practice. When we give thanks, we shift our focus from *what's missing to what's already been given.*

Jesus modeled this beautifully. Standing before a hungry crowd of thousands, with only five loaves and two fish, He didn't panic — He gave thanks.

> *"Then Jesus took the loaves, gave thanks to God, and distributed them to the people. Afterward he did the same with the fish. And they all ate as much as they wanted."*
> *~John 6:11 (NLT)*

The miracle didn't happen after Jesus asked — it happened after He thanked. Gratitude became the doorway to abundance.

That's what gratitude does: it multiplies what you have instead of magnifying what you lack.

The Quiet Power of Thankfulness

When Paul wrote from a Roman prison, he didn't say, *"Rejoice when you're released."* He wrote,

> *"Rejoice in the Lord always." (Philippians 4:4 NLT)*

He wasn't rejoicing in his situation — he was rejoicing in his Savior.

I've learned that gratitude changes the atmosphere of the heart. When you're tempted to focus on what didn't happen, gratitude whispers, *"But look what did."* When worry starts to spiral, gratitude interrupts it with remembrance.

Sometimes it's as simple as stopping to breathe a prayer:

Thank You, Lord, that I woke up today.

Thank You that You are near.

Thank you, that you still see me.

Thank You that You are still writing my story.

That's not denial — it's devotion.

Principles for the Journey

Gratitude is practiced, not just felt — and it teaches us to see God's goodness in what we once overlooked.

1. GRATITUDE REWIRES YOUR FOCUS

Gratitude begins with where you direct your attention. When your mind is shaped by truth, your heart becomes shaped by peace.

"Fix your thoughts on what is true, and honorable, and right, and pure, and lovely, and admirable."
~ Philippians 4:8 (NLT)

Whatever you focus on grows. When you fix your gaze on God's faithfulness, your fears begin to shrink.

2. GRATITUDE MULTIPLIES WHAT YOU HAVE

Gratitude doesn't wait for the blessing to appear. It starts with what's already in your hands and trusts God to do the rest.

"Then he took the seven loaves, thanked God for them, and broke them into pieces."
~ Mark 8:6 (NLT)

Jesus thanked God before the miracle, showing us that thanksgiving precedes increase.

3. GRATITUDE PROTECTS YOUR HEART FROM BITTERNESS

Bitterness grows in unguarded places, but gratitude is a shield that keeps your heart soft and your spirit steady.

"Let the peace that comes from Christ rule in your hearts. And always be thankful."
~ Colossians 3:15 (NLT)

Thankfulness is spiritual armor — it guards your peace when life tries to steal it.

4. GRATITUDE INVITES GOD'S PRESENCE

Gratitude is more than a feeling — it's an invitation.

"Enter his gates with thanksgiving; go into his courts with praise."
~ Psalm 100:4 (NLT)

Gratitude opens the door for God to dwell close. Where thankfulness is present, so is His peace.

5. GRATITUDE TURNS PAIN INTO PERSPECTIVE

Gratitude doesn't deny the pain, but it helps you see purpose within it. Trials look different when viewed through the lens of thankfulness.

"We can rejoice, too, when we run into problems and trials, for we know that they help us develop endurance."
~ Romans 5:3 (NLT)

When you learn to thank God in the storm, you begin to see growth where others see loss

Reflect & Apply

1. What's one thing you can thank God for today that you've recently overlooked?

2. How can gratitude change the way you view your current circumstances?

3. What practical step could you take this week to make gratitude a daily habit?

4. When have you experienced peace or joy after choosing gratitude over frustration?

5. How might your thankfulness encourage someone else who's struggling to see God's goodness?

Prayer

Father, thank You for every breath, every mercy, every unseen blessing. Teach me to see Your goodness in ordinary moments and to recognize Your provision even when life feels uncertain. Forgive me for the times I've focused on what's missing instead of what's present. Thank You that You still see me — fully, tenderly, completely. Give me a grateful heart that turns worry into worship and complaint into contentment. May my thankfulness draw others to You, the Giver of every good thing. Amen.

HOPE

THE ANCHOR OF THE SOUL

Last Light in Eder's Field

Dawn came slowly to Eder's Field, as if the sun itself hesitated to rise over the frost and silence. The sheep were huddled in the valley's low bowl, their breath rising in small, holy clouds. A single boy — Micah, son of no one remarkable — stood by the crumbling stone wall, his crook leaning against his shoulder, eyes fixed eastward where the hills glowed faintly with a promise he did not yet believe.

He had waited there every morning since the storm. His father's flock had been scattered; half lost to the wind, half to the wolves. The village said to move on — that nothing green would grow again in these fields. But Micah remembered the words his mother had spoken before her passing: *"If you tend what remains, Heaven will tend to the rest."*

So, he stayed.

The frost bit his fingers as he placed new seed in the soil. His knuckles were cracked, his tunic torn, and still he whispered a psalm beneath his breath — not for strength, but for patience. The hills seemed deaf to his prayer, but he prayed anyway, as if God were a shepherd too, counting His own stars in the dark.

Days passed. Weeks. The earth lay bare.

Then one morning — quiet, windless — he saw it: a single blade, thin as mercy, trembling in the dawn. It shimmered where the frost had melted, defiant against the cold. Micah fell to his knees. He did not cry out; he only bowed his head and smiled through the ache. Around him, the sheep began to stir. The valley breathed again.

By noon, the sun stood high, and the field glowed with faint color, as if the light itself remembered its duty. The boy rose, his shadow stretching long over the reborn soil.

Hope, he thought, *is not a thing that visits — it is a thing that waits with you.*

And above the field, unseen but certain, a lark took flight.

REFLECTION: HOPE THAT HOLDS

There's something sacred about that image — the boy standing in a frostbitten field, tending what remains while waiting for what will return. That's what hope does. It stays when reason walks away.

Hope doesn't ignore the storm; it simply refuses to be defined by it.

It's not a quick fix, nor a naïve optimism. It's the quiet decision to plant again, to show up again, to believe again — even when nothing has yet changed.

When I think of Micah in that field, I see the shape of what real hope looks like: cracked hands still working, weary eyes still watching, a heart still whispering prayers in the dark.

The writer of Hebrews captured this perfectly:

> *"This hope is a strong and trustworthy anchor for our souls. It leads us through the curtain into God's inner sanctuary."*
> *~ Hebrews 6:19 (NLT)*

An anchor doesn't remove the waves — it holds you steady through them. It's not glamorous; it's grounding. Hope keeps us from drifting when life's winds blow wild. It connects us, not to outcomes, but to God Himself.

When Waiting Becomes Worship

> Paul said, *"If we already have something, we don't need to hope for it. But if we look forward to something we don't yet have, we must wait patiently and confidently."*
> *~ Romans 8:24-25 (NLT)*

Hope lives in that tension — the not-yet, the middle ground between promise and fulfillment.

And yet, that middle ground is holy ground.

Like the boy in Eder's Field, we're often asked to tend barren places: to care for what's left, to keep faith alive when the evidence has gone missing. The secret of hope is this — it transforms waiting into worship. Every act of endurance becomes an offering; every prayer in the cold becomes a candle in the night.

I've had seasons where it felt like the sun was taking too long to rise — when prayers seemed unanswered and dreams felt dormant. But God was still working beneath the frost. Just because the field looks empty doesn't mean life isn't forming under the surface.

THE DAWN ALWAYS COMES

> David once wrote, *"Why am I discouraged? Why is my heart so sad? I will put my hope in God! I will praise Him again — my Savior and my God!"*
> *~ Psalm 42:11 (NLT)*

Notice that David's declaration of hope came before his breakthrough. He was still in the valley, still talking to himself — but he chose to preach to his own soul. That's what hope does: it reminds your spirit that dawn is coming, even while you're standing in the night.

Hope is not loud; it's loyal. It stays in the frost until the blade appears.

It holds onto God's faithfulness when everything else feels scattered.

And when that first green shoot appears — when the answer you've prayed for finally breaks the soil — hope bows its head in worship, because it knows Who sent the sunrise.

Principles for the Journey

Hope is the light that refuses to go out, even when the night feels endless.

1. **HOPE DOESN'T DENY REALITY — IT DEFINES IT THROUGH FAITH**

   Hope looks at the same circumstances everyone else sees but draws a different conclusion because it knows who holds the story.

   "We can rejoice, too, when we run into problems and trials, for we know that they help us develop endurance."
   ~ Romans 5:3 (NLT)

   Hope isn't pretending the pain isn't real. It's choosing to believe that the story isn't over.

2. **HOPE GROWS IN THE SOIL OF PERSISTENCE**

   Hope deepens every time you choose not to quit, even when progress seems invisible.

   "Let us hold tightly without wavering to the hope we affirm, for God can be trusted to keep His promise."
   ~ Hebrews 10:23 (NLT)

   Every time you keep showing up, even when you don't feel it, you're planting seeds for the next season's harvest.

3. HOPE ANCHORS THE SOUL WHEN CIRCUMSTANCES SHIFT

Hope settles your heart when life moves beneath your feet, reminding you that God never does.

"For You are my hope, O Sovereign Lord, my trust, O Lord, from my youth."
~ Psalm 71:5 (NLT)

When everything else drifts, hope ties you to God's character — steady, immovable, faithful.

4. HOPE IS STRENGTHENED THROUGH REMEMBRANCE

Hope rises when we look back and see the fingerprints of God all over our story.

"I remember the days of old. I ponder all your great works and think about what you have done."
~ Psalm 143:5 (NLT)

Remembering God's past faithfulness feeds your present faith.

5. HOPE AWAKENS OTHERS

Hope shines brightest when your faithfulness becomes the spark someone else needs to keep going.

"Let your light so shine before men, that they may see your good works and glorify your Father in heaven."
~ Matthew 5:16 (NLT)

When you hold onto hope, others find courage to keep believing too.

Reflect & Apply

1. What area of your life feels "frostbitten" right now — where you're waiting for signs of new growth?

2. How has God proven faithful in past seasons of waiting?

3. What helps you stay anchored when circumstances shift or prayers delay?

4. Who in your life might need to borrow your hope until they find their own again?

5. What "small act of tending" can you do this week to stay faithful where you are planted?

Father, thank You that hope is not a wish — it's a promise anchored in You. When life feels cold and prayers seem unanswered, remind me that You are still working beneath the surface. Teach me to wait with faith, to worship while I wait, and to tend what remains with love. Help me to be a light for others still standing in their own frost-covered fields. Let my hope point back to the sunrise only You can bring. Amen.

INTEGRITY

WHO YOU ARE WHEN NO ONE'S WATCHING

The Reluctant Builder

The sun hung low over the rolling hills as the builder wiped the sweat from his brow. For years, he had worked faithfully on the landowner's estate — crafting barns that stood against the wind, cottages that welcomed warmth, and stables that smelled faintly of cedar and straw.

He had poured his heart into every project, working with pride and precision. The landowner was kind, fair, and generous. But the builder was getting older now, his hands slower, his back heavier. He was ready to rest.

One morning, the landowner called him to the great house and said, “My friend, I have one more request before you retire. Would you build one last cottage for me?”

The builder smiled politely, though inwardly he sighed. *Another one?* he thought. *After all these years, can’t someone else do it?* Still, he nodded in agreement.

But this time was different. His heart wasn’t in it.

He took shortcuts. He used cheaper materials. He skipped the extra nails that kept the beams steady and ignored the hairline cracks that should have been repaired. The cottage looked fine on the outside — tidy walls, fresh paint, and a roof that shone under the sun — but inside, it lacked the care and craftsmanship of his best work.

When the last stone was laid and the door hung on its hinges, the builder stood back, ready to be done.

The landowner came to inspect the cottage. He walked slowly through each room, running his hand along the imperfect seams, saying nothing. When he returned to the builder, he smiled and handed him a small, wrapped box.

“This,” the landowner said softly, “is my gift to you — for all your years of service.”

The builder opened the box. Inside was a single brass key.

“It’s yours,” the landowner said. “This is your home.”

The builder froze. His breath caught in his chest as the truth sank in. The house he had built carelessly — the one where he had cut corners and saved himself time — was the very house he would now live in.

He bowed his head, shame and sorrow mixing in his heart. “If I had only known...” he whispered.

The landowner placed a hand on his shoulder. “I asked for your best,” he said gently. “Not for my sake — but for yours.”

Reflection: The House We Build Within

Integrity is the house we build when no one's looking. It's the unseen beams that hold our lives together — the daily decisions, the private words, the hidden motives. We're all building something, one choice at a time.

The question is: What kind of house are we building when no one will inspect it?

In the end, the life we construct in secret becomes the life we inhabit in public. The character we develop behind closed doors eventually defines the person everyone sees.

Scripture says,

> *"The integrity of the upright guides them, but the unfaithful are destroyed by their duplicity."*
> *~ Proverbs 11:3 (NLT)*

Integrity doesn't make you perfect — it makes you consistent. It's the alignment between what you believe and how you behave. It's when your heart and your habits speak the same truth.

There's a quiet beauty to integrity. It doesn't demand attention. It doesn't chase approval. It simply stands, steady and silent, when everything else shakes.

When David prayed, "Search me, O God, and know my heart," (Psalm 139:23 NLT), he wasn't asking for exposure; he was asking for alignment. That's the heart of integrity — to live open before God, knowing He sees what no one else does.

Because in the end, every wall we raise, every word we speak, every act we choose — we're building not just our reputation, but our soul.

Integrity in the Quiet Places

When Jesus was tempted in the wilderness, no one was watching. There were no crowds to applaud His restraint, no disciples to cheer Him on. Just silence, sand, and the whisper of compromise.

Yet, He stood firm. He chose truth over ease. Faithfulness over fame. Integrity over illusion.

The same is true for us. The quiet tests reveal the truest version of who we are. How we treat the unseen moments — the private thought, the small promise, the little compromise — determines whether our character will weather the storm.

Integrity is a daily construction project. The nails are honesty. The beams are humility. The foundation is trust. And the blueprint? God's Word.

Principles for the Journey

Integrity is the unseen work that builds the life you'll one day have to live in.

1. INTEGRITY IS BUILT ONE DECISION AT A TIME

Integrity begins in the quiet moment before the choice is made.

"People with integrity walk safely, but those who follow crooked paths will slip and fall."
~ Proverbs 10:9 (NLT)

Each small choice becomes a brick in the life you live. Build wisely.

2. INTEGRITY IS WHO YOU ARE WHEN NO ONE'S WATCHING

The unseen moments reveal the truth we often hide from ourselves.

"I will lead a life of integrity in my own home."
~ Psalm 101:2 (NLT)

Private righteousness is the seed of public credibility.

3. INTEGRITY REQUIRES HONESTY WITH YOURSELF

Only when we stop running from our motives can God begin to reshape them.

"Search me, O God, and know my heart; test me and know my anxious thoughts."
~ Psalm 139:23 (NLT)

When you let God examine your motives, He strengthens your foundation.

4. INTEGRITY COSTS YOU SOMETHING — BUT COMPROMISE COSTS MORE

There will always be an easier road — but rarely a better one.

"Better to be poor and honest than to be dishonest and rich."
~ Proverbs 19:1 (NLT)

Integrity may feel expensive in the moment, but it pays eternal dividends.

5. INTEGRITY IS A REFLECTION OF GOD'S CHARACTER

Every choice either mirrors His heart or masks it.

"Be holy in everything you do, just as God who chose you is holy."
~ 1 Peter 1:15 (NLT)

When you walk in truth, you mirror the heart of your Creator.

Reflect & Apply

1. What "house" are you building through your daily choices? Is it one you would want to live in?

2. When was the last time your integrity was tested in private? How did you respond?

3. What areas of your life need reinforcement — where compromise has started to creep in?

4. How can you make integrity your daily habit rather than a heroic act?

5. If your life were the cottage in this story, what would you want the Landowner to find when He opens the door?

Father, thank You for seeing not just what I do, but who I am becoming. Teach me to build my life with care and conviction. Help me honor You in the quiet places, where the applause is silent but the reward eternal. When temptation whispers that shortcuts are harmless, remind me that You are both my builder and my blueprint. Let my life be a house of truth, where Your presence feels at home. Amen.

JOY

THE CALM DELIGHT OF TRUSTING GOD

Blessed Assurance

The sun was already slipping low when Mom's AMC Gremlin turned onto our dusty street. She had just finished a long shift at Midland Memorial Hospital, the soft blue of her uniform wrinkled from hours on her feet. I sat in the passenger seat, still in my school clothes, my three-ring notebook and math book stacked in my lap.

"What's for supper?" I asked as we passed the grocery store.

Mom smiled gently and said, "The Lord will provide."

Her voice carried no strain, only the calm certainty of someone who had said it before — and seen it proven true. As the hum of the tires filled the car, she began to sing softly under her breath:

"Blessed assurance, Jesus is mine ... "

The melody wrapped around us like sunlight through clouds. Her voice was weary, but sure — an echo of joy that didn't depend on circumstance.

After Dad passed away there had been seasons when the world seemed unbearably heavy. Yet Mom never let sorrow have the final word. She had learned to let joy lead, even when the cupboards were empty, even when the bills waited by the door.

That afternoon, I watched her hands on the steering wheel — steady, strong, graceful. The kind of strength that doesn't shout, it just sings.

When we pulled into the garage and walked toward the front door, the smell of rain lingered in the air. Mom's humming hadn't stopped.

Then we saw it — sitting quietly on the porch, as if God Himself had made a delivery: a large box filled with canned goods, potatoes, soups, and potted meats. There was enough to last until payday.

I turned to Mom, wide-eyed. "Who do you think did this?"

She smiled, the kind of smile that comes from deep wells of faith. "The Lord did," she said softly. Then she placed her hand on my shoulder and added, "Joy keeps a light in the window so we never miss the ways God provides."

That night, the house was full — not just of food, but of the sound of her joy filled song drifting down the hall. It wasn't a victory shout; it was something better — a calm delight in a faithful God.

Reflection: Joy Is the Song That Never Goes Silent

Joy doesn't wait for circumstances to change. It changes the atmosphere around you until you can see God in it.

My mother didn't sing because life was easy. She sang because she had learned that praise and peace share the same key.

Paul said,

> *"Always be full of joy in the Lord. I say it again — rejoice!"*
> *~ Philippians 4:4 (NLT)*

He wrote those words from a prison cell. No comfort. No guarantees. But his heart was free because his focus was fixed. That's the secret of joy — it's not built on what's happening around you, but on Who's living within you.

Joy is the steady rhythm of trust that keeps your faith from falling out of tune.

It's the quiet melody that says, God hasn't failed me yet, and He won't start now.

The Strength Hidden in Joy

Nehemiah said it best:

> *"Don't be dejected and sad, for the joy of the Lord*
> *is your strength."*
> *~ Nehemiah 8:10 (NLT)*

Joy is strength disguised as song. It gives you the ability to stand when life bends you low.

Mom's joy wasn't loud, but it was unshakable. It didn't deny hardship; it defined it — turning the ordinary moments of lack into sacred spaces where God could move.

Even now, when I hum that same hymn — "Blessed assurance, Jesus is mine" — I'm reminded that joy is not about ignoring pain;

it's about inviting God into it. Because joy isn't the absence of hardship — it's the presence of God's faithfulness in the middle of it.

Storms don't silence joy — they give it room to echo.

Principles for the Journey

Joy is the sacred strength that rises not from circumstance, but from the presence of God within us.

1. JOY STARTS WITH PRESENCE, NOT PLENTY

Joy begins the moment your heart becomes aware that God is nearer than your need.

"You will show me the way of life, granting me the joy of Your presence."
~ Psalm 16:11 (NLT)

When you know Who walks with you, you stop worrying about what's missing.

2. JOY TRANSFORMS HARDSHIP INTO WORSHIP

Joy rises in the very places where pain tries to silence your praise.

"We are sorrowful, yet always rejoicing."
~ 2 Corinthians 6:10 (NLT)

When you sing in the storm, you're declaring that God's goodness is greater than your need.

3. JOY IS SUSTAINED BY GRATITUDE

Joy grows when you choose to notice the gifts that are already in your hands.

"Be thankful in all circumstances, for this is God's will for you who belong to Christ Jesus."
~ 1 Thessalonians 5:18 (NLT)

Gratitude is the soil where joy takes root and grows.

4. JOY STRENGTHENS THE WEARY HEART

Joy becomes power when everything in you feels too tired to take another step.

"The joy of the Lord is your strength."
~ Nehemiah 8:10 (NLT)

When faith feels fragile, joy becomes the anchor that steadies you.

5. JOY INVITES DIVINE PROVISION

Joy creates space for God to move in ways you weren't expecting.

"This is the day the Lord has made. We will rejoice and be glad in it."
~ Psalm 118:24 (NLT)

Joy opens the door for God's timing and favor — it creates an atmosphere for miracles.

Reflect & Apply

1. What does "the joy of the Lord is your strength" look like in your life right now?

2. When have you seen joy shift the atmosphere in a difficult moment?

3. What "song" or scripture do you turn to when life feels heavy?

4. How can you practice gratitude today as a pathway to greater joy?

5. Think of one person who needs encouragement — how can your joy become their reminder of God's faithfulness?

Prayer

Lord, thank You for the melody of joy that plays even when life feels uncertain. Teach me to hum praise instead of worry. Let Your presence be my assurance when I cannot see provision yet. Fill my home, my heart, and my habits with songs of trust. And when storms come, let my faith remember this: You are still good, and You are still here. Amen.

KINDNESS

TURNING COMPASSION INTO ACTION

The Man by the Murphy Station

The late-morning sun was already hot that day in Bowie, Texas. The kind of heat that makes the asphalt shimmer and the air hum. I'd stopped at the Murphy gas station by Walmart — a place I visited often — to fill up before heading home for a Teams conference call with colleagues. I was cutting it close; it takes about twenty-five minutes to get home, and the clock was already working against me.

That's when I saw him.

He sat on a big landscaping rock at the corner where the parking lot meets the road — a weathered man in a faded Army cap, his belongings packed neatly beside him. He held a cardboard sign, handwritten and simple:

"Vet. Hungry. Will work for food."

It was a scene I'd passed before, at other intersections, other towns. But something in his stillness caught me. Maybe it was the quiet dignity in how he sat, or the way he didn't wave the sign, just held it gently, like a last piece of truth he still believed in.

As I pulled out from the station, I felt a nudge — not loud, but clear as a bell in my spirit:

"Give him some food."

I wish I could say I turned the car around immediately. But instead, I argued.

"I've got a meeting."

"I'm already late."

"Somebody else can help."

Half a mile later, the excuses fell silent — replaced by that unmistakable heaviness in my gut that I've come to recognize as conviction.

I turned the car around.

Back in the Walmart lot, I parked and walked inside, bought a sandwich from the deli, a bag of chips, and a bottle of cold water. Simple. Quick. Exactly what the Spirit had said.

When I pulled up beside him, he looked up with tired eyes that still managed a smile. I stepped out, holding out the bag. "Hey, thought you might need something to eat."

He took it with both hands — gentle, careful — and said quietly, "Thank you, sir."

I asked how he was getting along. He said, "Day to day. Just trying to make it to Amarillo. My family's up there."

We talked for a few minutes. Then I asked if I could pray with him. Right there on the corner — Walmart on one side, cars rushing by on the other — we bowed our heads. I prayed that God would protect him, provide for him, and get him safely to his family.

When I said amen, he looked up and said softly, "I needed that. God bless you."

I smiled and told him, "He already has."

As I drove away, the strangest thing happened — that familiar anxiety about my meeting melted into peace. I made it home, logged on right at the scheduled time... only to find out the call had been postponed.

I laughed out loud. God had rearranged the day, not to inconvenience me, but to invite me.

I've never seen that man again. I've often wondered if he made it to Amarillo — or if, perhaps, he was an angel sent to test a lesson I keep learning: **kindness is obedience in motion.**

The Sacred Interruptions

Kindness rarely arrives when it's convenient.

It comes as an interruption — a moment where heaven slips into your schedule and asks, "Will you stop long enough to love?"

I almost missed that moment. But when I turned around, something in me turned too.

Paul wrote,

> *"Be kind to each other, tenderhearted, forgiving one another, just as God through Christ has forgiven you."*
> *~ Ephesians 4:32 (NLT)*

Kindness doesn't wait for permission. It moves. It notices. It acts.

Jesus told stories about seeds and soil, about lamps and neighbors — but every one of them was really about love in action. Kindness is how love gets its hands dirty. It's how compassion becomes visible.

And when we obey those small promptings — even in parking lots and passing moments — something divine happens. The giver and the receiver both walk away changed.

WHAT KINDNESS TEACHES THE HEART

Kindness isn't weakness. It's wisdom wrapped in gentleness.

It teaches us that obedience is often quieter than we expect — not a sermon, but a sandwich; not a grand gesture, but a few minutes given away in the name of mercy.

Sometimes I think about that day and realize the miracle wasn't that I turned around — it's that God was patient enough to wait for me to.

Kindness has that effect: it doesn't just change the one who receives it; it transforms the one who gives it.

Proverbs 11:25 says,

> *"The generous will prosper; those who refresh others will themselves be refreshed." (NLT)*

That's exactly what I felt on that drive home — refreshed. Filled. Peaceful. Because when you obey God's promptings, even in the smallest things, He takes care of the rest.

Principles for the Journey

Kindness is the courage to step in a new direction when God redirects your path.

1. KINDNESS BEGINS WITH LISTENING

The first movement of kindness is not action, but attention.

"Don't look out only for your own interests, but take an interest in others, too."
~ Philippians 2:4 (NLT)

Sometimes the Spirit's whisper is the first act of compassion.

2. KINDNESS COSTS SOMETHING REAL

True kindness always asks you to give up a little comfort so someone else can breathe again.

"If someone has enough money to live well and sees a brother or sister in need but shows no compassion — how can God's love be in that person?"
~ 1 John 3:17 (NLT)

The inconvenience is part of the offering.

3. KINDNESS RESTORES DIGNITY

Every act of kindness lifts a bowed head a little higher.

"Love is patient and kind."
~ 1 Corinthians 13:4 (NLT)

Kindness doesn't just feed a need; it restores worth.

4. KINDNESS INVITES DIVINE TIMING

When you choose compassion over convenience, you make room for God to rearrange the moment.

"Give, and you will receive. Your gift will return to you in full ..."
~ Luke 6:38 (NLT)

When your priorities align with God's heart, He handles your calendar.

5. KINDNESS IS WORSHIP IN DISGUISE

Each gentle act becomes a quiet echo of the mercy that once rescued you.

"But when the kindness and love of God our Savior appeared, He saved us."
~ Titus 3:4-5 (NLT)

Every act of compassion is a small echo of salvation — love showing up again.

Reflect & Apply

1. Have you ever felt God prompting you to show kindness but hesitated? What held you back?

2. How can you learn to see interruptions as divine invitations rather than inconveniences?

3. What does it mean to you that kindness is "obedience in motion"?

4. Who might be sitting at the "corner of your day" right now — waiting for your compassion?

5. How could you make space in your daily routine to act on those small nudges from the Spirit?

Prayer

Lord, thank You for every moment You interrupt my plans with Yours. Teach me to pause long enough to notice the need right in front of me. When my heart reaches for excuses, remind me that kindness is obedience in motion. Use me to refresh others, and let the peace that follows be the quiet reward of walking with You. And whenever You place someone on the path of my day, may they see Your love reflected in the way I choose to serve. Amen.

LOVE

THE FOUNDATION OF EVERY POSITIVE MINDSET

Love Stops on Southlake Boulevard

It was evening, and Christine and I were on our way to meet her sister, Tamra, and brother-in-law, Bill, for dinner near Southlake, Texas. The air outside was still warm from the day — that golden Texas dusk that makes even traffic lights look forgiving.

We were deep in conversation, talking about life, work, and family — the kind of talk that makes miles melt away. That's probably why I didn't notice the gas gauge sitting squarely on *E*.

As we approached the intersection where Southlake Boulevard meets 377 in Keller, the light turned red. We stopped, third lane from the right, surrounded by a river of headlights. When the light turned green, our car sputtered, coughed ... and died.

Right there. In rush-hour traffic.

Instantly, the world erupted in sound — horns blaring, engines growling, voices shouting things best left unrepeated. Christine glanced at me, calm but concerned.

"Put it in neutral," I said, trying to sound steady. "I'll push."

She slid to the driver's seat while I stepped out, the humid air thick with exhaust and frustration. I got behind the car and pushed. But we were on a slight incline — and the car started to roll backward.

Now, picture this: a 350-pound man in business clothes, huffing behind a full-size sedan trying to fight physics on an uphill slope. My feet slipped, my lungs burned, my shirt was already sticking to me. Somewhere behind me a driver leaned on their horn like they were auditioning for a traffic symphony.

Just as I was deciding whether this was the day my obituary might read *"stranded in Keller, Texas"* — Tamra came running across three lanes of traffic toward us.

Bill stayed in their SUV with the hazard lights blinking like a guardian angel on wheels. But Tamra — God bless her — was right there with me, pushing the car, laughing between gasps.

"Mike," she said, "I don't know how much longer I can do this!"

"Me neither!" I wheezed.

We were both laughing and praying at the same time, trying not to die of exhaustion or embarrassment. And despite all our effort, the car wasn't moving.

That's when I whispered, "God, I need some help here."

Before I could even take another breath, help arrived.

Out of nowhere, a man appeared behind us. No words, no hesitation — he simply placed both hands on the trunk beside mine and said, "Let's get this car to that parking lot."

His voice carried calm authority, the kind that makes you believe it's already done.

"Christine, steer right!" I called.

Together we pushed — three lanes of moving traffic, headlights parting as though heaven was making room. Somehow, we made it to a parking lot at the corner.

When we finally stopped, I leaned against the car, out of breath, drenched, but grateful. Tamra was laughing again, that "I can't believe we just did that" kind of laugh.

I turned to the man. "Thank you for stopping," I said. "Everyone else just drove by."

He smiled — quiet, almost shy. "It was nothing."

I shook my head. "No," I said. "It was something. It was an act of love."

He nodded once and walked off into the night.

To this day, I don't know where he came from or where he went. But I know what he represented.

Because that night, on Southlake Boulevard — **love stopped**.

Love Stops

Love doesn't wait for perfect conditions. It steps into the mess of the moment.

It doesn't calculate what it will cost; it simply asks, *"Who needs me right now?"*

> *"Let all that you do be done in love."*
> *~ 1 Corinthians 16:14 (NLT)*

That night wasn't just about a car in traffic; it was about a reminder. Love shows up where impatience lives. It finds room in crowded places. It pushes through when you've got nothing left.

And sometimes, it shows up in work boots and disappears before you can say thank you.

The Foundation of Every Positive Mindset

Love is the root system of the renewed mind. It feeds everything else — patience, kindness, faith, and joy. Remove love, and even good works grow hollow.

Jesus said,

> *"You must love the Lord your God with all your heart, all your soul, and all your mind. This is the first and greatest commandment. A second is equally important: Love your neighbor as yourself."*
> *~ Matthew 22:37-39 (NLT)*

Love is not just God's command — it's His character.

When you love — even when it's inconvenient or exhausting — you align with His very nature.

That night, as Christine and I sat in the car catching our breath, I remember saying softly, "We're okay."

And in my spirit, I heard the echo: Yes — because love showed up.

What Love Teaches Us

> *"Dear friends, let us continue to love one another, for love comes from God."*
> *~ 1 John 4:7 (NLT)*

Love teaches us that the greatest miracles often happen in ordinary places — intersections and parking lots. It reminds us that a simple act of compassion can carry eternal weight.

And maybe — just maybe — the man who helped us that night was more than he appeared.

Because sometimes, angels still walk Southlake Boulevard.

Principles for the Journey

Love is the force that steps into the chaos, steadies the moment, and reminds us that heaven still breaks into ordinary places.

1. LOVE MOVES FIRST

Love slips into the room softly, yet its presence rewrites the moment.

"We love each other because He loved us first."
~ 1 John 4:19 (NLT)

Before we ever take a step toward someone else, God has already taken a step toward us. His love initiates ours.

2. LOVE INTERRUPTS YOUR PLANS

Love rewrites the moment, pulling your attention from what you were doing to who is right in front of you.

"Love is patient and kind."
~ 1 Corinthians 13:4 (NLT)

Real love slows down, makes room, and chooses kindness — even when it means changing your schedule.

3. LOVE CROSSES DANGEROUS LANES

Sometimes love draws a line between what's safe and what's needed — and invites you to stand in the gap.

"Love covers a multitude of sins."
~ 1 Peter 4:8 (NLT)

Love risks comfort and convenience to reach others, offering grace instead of judgment.

4. LOVE CHANGES BOTH THE GIVER AND THE RECEIVER

Whenever love flows through you, it leaves an imprint — quiet, deep, and unmistakably holy.

"Give, and you will receive. Your gift will return to you in full ... "
~ Luke 6:38 (NLT)

Every act of love transforms two lives — the one who gives it and the one who receives it.

5. LOVE LEAVES FINGERPRINTS OF HEAVEN

Love lingers in a room long after the moment has passed, like a light that refuses to fade.

"The greatest of these is love."
~ 1 Corinthians 13:13 (NLT)

Love is the evidence of God at work in us; it's the mark of His presence in the world.

Reflect & Apply

1. When has someone "stopped" for you in a moment of need?

2. What keeps you from showing love when life gets busy or loud?

3. How can you treat interruptions as divine appointments?

4. Who in your life needs you to "cross the lanes" for them right now?

5. How does love — both given and received — change the way you see God's timing?

Prayer

Lord, help me to notice the moments where love wants to stop. When I see someone stranded — literally or spiritually — give me the courage to act. When I am the one stalled in traffic, send someone filled with Your Spirit to help me move again. Teach me that love is never wasted, and that even in the middle of life's noise, You are the God who shows up right on time. Amen.

MINDFULNESS

BE PRESENT, NOTICE GOD IN THE MOMENT

The Whisper Beneath the Noise

Working remote, it was one of those mornings when everything moved too fast. Emails were piling up, my phone buzzed without mercy, and meeting reminders flashed across the corner of my screen like impatient traffic lights. The world outside my office window was calm, but inside — it felt like rush hour in my mind.

At some point, I caught my own reflection in the dark screen of my 40-inch monitor — tired eyes, tight shoulders, shallow breathing. My body was in the chair, but my spirit was miles away.

I thought about my sister, Jeanette, who's now with the Lord. She used to tell me when life came at you ninety miles an hour, *"Just breathe in Jesus."*

Even though she's gone, her words live on — and on a day like today, that's exactly what I needed to do.

I leaned back in my chair, closed my eyes, and took a slow, deliberate breath.

Outside, a breeze stirred through the small trees in our front yard. Sunlight slipped through the blinds and danced across my office floor. The hum of the computer softened, and for a moment, the noise of the world faded into the quiet of His presence.

In that stillness, I sensed it — not an audible voice, but a whisper within:

> *"Be still, and know that I am God."*
> *~ Psalm 46:10 (NLT)*

It wasn't correction; it was an invitation — a reminder that God wasn't waiting at the end of my day to meet me after the chaos cleared. He was already here, breathing peace into the spaces I had filled with noise.

Mindfulness in the Christian life isn't about emptying your mind. It's about filling it — with awareness of the One who is already near.

When We Rush Past God

We often assume God meets us only in big moments — special services, answered prayers, major breakthroughs. But He's also in the quiet ones: the smell of morning coffee, a kind text that arrives right when you need it, the hush between meetings when your thoughts finally slow.

Sometimes the enemy's most effective tactic isn't temptation — it's acceleration.

If he can't make us sin, he'll make us busy. Because when we rush, we stop noticing the holy hidden in the ordinary.

Jesus never hurried. Crowds pressed in on every side, yet He remained grounded in divine awareness. He noticed what others missed — the woman who touched His robe, the children everyone tried to shoo away, the sinner hiding in shame.

That's what mindfulness does: it restores sight. It helps us see God not only in miracles but in *moments*.

Moments That Become Altars

There's a phrase that has stayed with me for years: *"Build altars where you notice God."*

Jacob did that after his dream of a ladder reaching into heaven. He woke in awe and said,

> *"Surely the Lord is in this place, and I wasn't even aware of it!"*
> *~ Genesis 28:16 (NLT)*

That's the heartbeat of mindfulness — recognizing the sacred woven into the ordinary.

When you pause and whisper, "Thank You, Lord — You're here," your home becomes a sanctuary.

Your commute becomes communion.

Your breath becomes worship.

You don't need to go somewhere else to meet God. You just need to look where you already are.

The Still Gift of the Present

We say "live in the moment," but Scripture calls it something deeper — abiding.

> *"Remain in Me, and I will remain in you."*
> *~John 15:4 (NLT)*

Abiding isn't about withdrawing from the world — it's about walking through it with awareness. It's not about control; it's about connection.

When you slow down long enough to breathe in His nearness, anxiety begins to loosen its grip.

When you start to listen instead of react, gratitude deepens its roots.

And peace — that rare, steady peace — quietly returns to its rightful place.

Because you don't have to control everything when you remember Who's already holding everything.

Principles for the Journey

Mindfulness is the grace that quiets the noise long enough for you to hear the God who never stopped speaking.

1. **MINDFULNESS HELPS YOU SLOW DOWN AND SEE GOD IN MOTION**

   Right before the day starts pressing in, God creates a small window where you can remember who holds the day.

   "Be still, and know that I am God.
   ~ Psalm 46:10 (NLT)

   Stillness isn't inactivity; it's intentional awareness of God's presence.

2. **MINDFULNESS BUILDS ALTARS WHERE YOU NOTICE HIS PRESENCE**

   Some moments slip by quietly, carrying a weight you only recognize when you choose to stop and honor them.

   "Surely the Lord is in this place, and I wasn't even aware of it."
   ~ Genesis 28:16 (NLT)

   Moments of awareness become memorials of faith.

3. MINDFULNESS RESTS YOUR MIND WHERE YOUR HEART ABIDES

When distractions quiet down, your heart remembers Who it belongs to.

"Remain in Me, and I will remain in you."
~ John 15:4 (NLT)

Peace is born from presence, not performance.

4. MINDFULNESS TRADES REACTION FOR REVELATION

When you quiet the inner storm, truth surfaces — not loud, but unmistakably clear.

"My sheep listen to My voice; I know them, and
they follow Me."
~ John 10:27 (NLT)

Listening always comes before leading.

5. MINDFULNESS REMINDS YOU THAT THE PRESENT MOMENT IS HOLY GROUND

When you slow down long enough to notice God, the ordinary moment becomes a meeting place with Him.

"Take off your sandals, for you are standing
on holy ground."
~ Exodus 3:5 (NLT)

Everywhere God is noticed, heaven touches earth.

Reflect & Apply

1. When was the last time you paused and truly noticed God's presence in your day?

2. What areas of your life feel too noisy to hear His whisper?

3. How might slowing down transform the way you experience His peace?

4. Where could you "build an altar" — a reminder of God's presence — in your daily routine?

5. What might happen if you began treating every moment as holy ground?

Prayer

Lord, still my restless thoughts. Help me to find You not only in the mountaintop moments but in the daily rhythms of life. Open my eyes to see Your hand in every small mercy — in sunlight, in laughter, in the silence between words. Teach me to walk slowly enough to notice Your presence and to build altars in ordinary places. Amen.

NOBLENESS

Fixing Your Thoughts on What Is Honorable

"Fix your thoughts on what is true, and honorable, and right, and pure, and lovely, and admirable. Think about things that are excellent and worthy of praise."
~ Philippians 4:8 (NLT)

The Quiet High Note

It began with an unexpected meeting request — a short message that appeared on my screen one morning between project updates and calendar reminders. When I clicked the link, my new supervisor appeared on the video call from Colorado. I'd never met her in person. Alongside her was an HR representative. Their expressions were polite, professional, and heavy with what I already sensed was coming.

"Mike," she said gently, "your position is being eliminated. The role is being transitioned to Malaysia."

The words landed like a quiet echo.

After nearly a decade with the company, the role I had built, refined, and poured my energy into was being relocated overseas. My responsibilities would be divided among three people — a supervisor in Colorado, a resource in Malaysia, and a team member I had trained years earlier in Korea.

They gave me ninety days. Ninety days to close out more than forty projects, document years of processes, and train the team members who would carry on the work.

If I completed everything, I'd receive severance through the end of the year. If not, I'd lose it.

For a moment, I just sat there — still on the call, nodding, thanking them for the information. After the meeting ended, I stared at the blank screen for a long time.

Ten years of work... and a ninety-day countdown to closure.

It was a strange season of life — one that made me reflect on both the years behind me and the ones still ahead. Many at my age begin to think about slowing down, about stepping away. But I didn't feel done. I still loved the work — the creating, the teaching, the building. I wasn't ready to retire; I still felt called to contribute, to mentor, to help others grow.

So, I took a few days to pray, to breathe, and to ask God to help me end this chapter with grace. When I came back, I made a quiet promise: *If this was how it ended, it was going to end well.*

I began to write — documenting every process, every workflow, every lesson learned. I trained the supervisor in Colorado on systems and strategies she'd never seen before. I met with the resource in Malaysia to build bridges across cultures and time zones. And I spent late nights on calls with my former trainee in Korea — showing her not just the "how," but the "why." Years earlier, I had trained her to design learning materials. Now I was teaching her how to configure systems, manage content, and lead.

It wasn't easy. Some days the silence was heavy, the work exhausting. But I kept hearing a still, small voice whisper, *Do this unto Me.*

When my final day came, everything was done — every task completed, every deliverable finished, every process carefully passed on. My supervisor scheduled a final call.

"Mike," she said, "you've exceeded expectations. You didn't just hand things off — you built a framework for success. That speaks volumes about your character."

When the call ended, I sat quietly in my office. No applause, no farewell cake, no audience. Just the soft hum of the computer and a deep sense of peace.

It wasn't pride I felt — it was gratitude. Gratitude that God had given me strength to finish with integrity, and that I could walk away with my heart clean.

That peace had a name.

Nobleness.

The Meaning of Nobleness

In Philippians 4:8, Paul writes,

> *"Fix your thoughts on what is true, and honorable, and right, and pure, and lovely, and admirable." (NLT)*

The word translated "honorable" here is the Greek word **σεμνός (semnos)** — meaning *noble, dignified, worthy of respect, reverent in character.*

It describes a mindset that lives above reproach, not in arrogance, but in steady resolve — the kind of inner stability that shines when life shakes you.

Nobleness is not about status or title. It's about *stewardship* — tending to what's been entrusted to you, even when no one is watching. It's the posture of a heart that says, I *will still do what's right, because it honors God.*

"Nobleness is not found in recognition, but in reflection — when your actions mirror the quiet dignity of Christ."

Principles for the Journey

Nobleness is the unwavering character that holds its ground when life shifts beneath your feet, choosing what honors God even when no one sees.

1. NOBLENESS BEGINS IN THE MIND

Every noble life begins with a choice — to direct your thoughts toward what honors God instead of what your emotions naturally pull toward.

"Fix your thoughts ... "
~ Philippians 4:8 (NLT)

Paul's instruction to "fix your thoughts" isn't passive — it's intentional. We train our minds to dwell on what honors God, and that alignment produces peace.

2. NOBLENESS IS REVEALED THROUGH INTEGRITY UNDER PRESSURE

When the weight of uncertainty presses down, nobleness stands taller — not by strength, but by conviction.

"The integrity of the upright guides them, but the unfaithful are destroyed by their duplicity."
~ Proverbs 11:3 (NLT)

Integrity isn't proven when things go well — it's forged when everything feels uncertain. The noble mind stays anchored in truth, even when comfort would be easier.

3. NOBLENESS EXPRESSES GRACE WHEN OTHERS EXPECT RESENTMENT

Grace becomes noble when it shows up in the very place where bitterness feels deserved.

"Since I, your Lord and Teacher, have washed your feet, you ought to wash each other's feet."
~John 13:14 (NLT)

Jesus modeled what it means to serve those who may not understand the cost of your sacrifice. Nobleness doesn't lash out; it leans down to lift others.

4. NOBLENESS WALKS HUMBLY WITH GOD

True nobleness is the quiet consistency of choosing God's way over your own, one unseen step at a time.

"The Lord has told you what is good... to do what is right, to love mercy, and to walk humbly with your God."
~ Micah 6:8 (NLT)

True nobleness isn't self-made. It's born from walking with God in the small, unseen moments — the steady faithfulness that leaves a legacy long after your role changes.

5. NOBLENESS IS THE QUIET COURAGE TO DO WHAT'S RIGHT WHEN NO ONE'S APPLAUDING

Nobleness is revealed in the unseen moments, where obedience becomes worship and excellence becomes your offering to God.

> *"So let's not get tired of doing what is good. At just the right time we will reap a harvest of blessing if we don't give up."*
> *~ Galatians 6:9 (NLT)*

Decide to choose peace over pride, service over resentment, and integrity over self-interest. It's the grace to finish well — not because you have to, but because that's who you are in Christ.

Reflect & Apply

1. When have you had to finish strong in a season of transition or uncertainty?

2. What does it look like to "fix your thoughts" on what is honorable when life feels unfair?

3. How can you show grace in a space where you once felt dismissed or overlooked?

4. What would it mean for your work — or your waiting — to reflect the heart of *semnos*, nobleness before God?

5. What is one quiet, noble choice you can make this week that no one but God will see?

Father, thank you for calling me to a life marked by nobleness. Teach me to guard my thoughts, to walk humbly, and to respond with grace even when life feels unfair. Strengthen me to finish well in every assignment You give me — whether or not anyone sees. Let my actions reflect Your character, and let my heart remain anchored in what is true and honorable. Amen.

OBEDIENCE

THE BLESSING OF A SIMPLE YES

"Behold, to obey is better than sacrifice, and to heed is better than the fat of rams."
~ 1 Samuel 15:22 (NLT)

The Whisper That Moved Heaven

It happened in the early days of Jesus' ministry — shortly after His baptism in the Jordan, His testing in the wilderness, and the first steps of calling the men who would walk with Him. The dust of Israel was still fresh on His sandals when He found Himself at a wedding in Cana — a celebration filled with laughter, music, and the warmth of family gathering.

But beneath the joy of the feast, a quiet crisis was unfolding: **the wine had run out**.

Mary saw it first. She turned to Jesus with a simple observation: **"They have no more wine."**

His reply was gentle, but firm: **"Dear woman, that's not our problem. My time has not yet come."**

And yet Mary sensed something the moment couldn't quite hold. She turned — not to Jesus, but to the servants standing nearby — and offered the whisper that would move Heaven: **"Do whatever He tells you."**

Six stone jars stood waiting. Nothing about them looked miraculous. But when Jesus spoke — "Fill the jars with water" — the servants obeyed without hesitation. They filled them to the brim.

And that's when it happened.

The miracle wasn't about wine — it was about willingness.

It wasn't about what was inside the jars, but about the hearts of the people willing to fill them.

Jesus could have spoken the wine into existence, but He invited ordinary hands into an extraordinary moment. Their obedience became the bridge between His instruction and His intervention. They didn't understand the logic; they simply trusted the Lord they barely knew.

And because they obeyed, they witnessed wonder.

When the master of ceremonies tasted the water-turned-wine, he declared it the finest of the feast. Heaven had touched earth — not with noise or spectacle, but through a simple act of surrender.

The Hidden Power of Obedience

Obedience is one of Scripture's simplest commands — and one of life's hardest disciplines.

It demands trust before clarity, action before assurance.

When Saul tried to substitute partial obedience with religious performance, Samuel corrected him sharply:

> *"Obedience is better than sacrifice."*
> *~ 1 Samuel 15:22 (NLT)*

God values alignment over appearance. Sacrifice impresses men; obedience pleases God. Even Jesus modeled this.

Philippians 2:8 (NLT) says:

> *"He humbled Himself in obedience to God and died a criminal's death on a cross."*

> *"Though sinless, He learned obedience through the things He suffered"*
> *~ Hebrews 5:8 (NLT)*

Every step of His earthly life was shaped by surrender to the Father's will.

Obedience doesn't always lead where we want to go — but it always leads us closer to God's heart.

Learning Through Surrender

Obedience is partnership with God.

He supplies the power; we supply the yes.

Like the servants at Cana, our obedience often seems small:

- *Forgive*
- *Go*
- *Give*
- *Speak*
- *Wait*
- *Be still*

These are simple commands, but they shape eternal outcomes.

In my own life, obedience has rarely felt convenient.

Sometimes it has cost reputation, comfort, or control.

But it has always brought peace — because peace belongs to those who move when God speaks, even when the path is unclear.

Obedience doesn't always make sense in the moment — but it always makes miracles in hindsight.

When God Interrupts Your Plan

Obedience often begins as an interruption.

Moses was tending sheep when God called him from a burning bush.

Peter was mending nets when Jesus said, "Follow Me."

Mary was living quietly when Gabriel said, "You will bear a Son."

Divine interruptions are invitations disguised as inconvenience.

When God disrupts your comfort, it's never to diminish your life — it's to redirect it.

The servants at Cana could have ignored Mary's words. They could have reasoned, *We need wine, not water.* But instead, they acted. And their obedience unlocked a miracle that still preaches centuries later.

So often we want God to show us His power before we step out, but Heaven's pattern is the reverse: *step first, then see.*

Principles for the Journey

Obedience is the simple yes that opens the door for God to do what only He can do.

1. OBEDIENCE REVEALS TRUST

Obedience speaks a language the heart can't fake — your actions declare what your lips may hesitate to say.

"If you love Me, obey My commandments."
~ John 14:15 (NLT)

Love proves itself not through emotion but through action.

2. OBEDIENCE PRECEDES UNDERSTANDING

God often invites you to move while the path is still dim, knowing clarity will meet you on the other side of your yes.

"We live by believing and not by seeing."
~ 2 Corinthians 5:7 (NLT)

Understanding often comes after the step of faith, not before it.

3. OBEDIENCE INVITES DIVINE PARTNERSHIP

God delights in taking your simple, ordinary step and weaving His power through it in ways you could never imagine.

"Fill the jars with water."
~ John 2:7 (NLT)

God uses our simple actions as vessels for His supernatural work.

4. OBEDIENCE TURNS ORDINARY MOMENTS INTO HOLY GROUND

A moment becomes sacred the instant you respond to God's voice, even if the place around you looks unchanged.

"Take off your sandals, for you are standing on
holy ground."
~ Exodus 3:5 (NLT)

When you move at His word, even a workplace, a car, or a kitchen can become a sanctuary.

5. OBEDIENCE TRANSFORMS SACRIFICE INTO SURRENDER

True sacrifice offers something to God; obedience offers *yourself.*

"Present your bodies as a living and holy sacrifice."
~ Romans 12:1 (NLT)

Just like the water in those jars, your surrendered yes becomes the very thing God transforms.

Reflect & Apply

1. When has obedience felt like an interruption in your life — but later revealed God's purpose?

2. What "jar" might God be asking you to fill right now, even if it doesn't make sense?

3. In what area do you struggle most to trust God's timing or instruction?

4. How might simple, consistent obedience open the door for a miracle in your current season?

5. What does it mean for you personally to turn sacrifice into surrender?

Prayer

Father, thank You for every whisper that calls me into obedience. Teach me to respond with trust even when I don't yet understand. When my logic resists Your leading, soften my heart to surrender. Let my willingness become the water You turn into wine. Fill my life with the joy of obedience and the blessing of a simple surrender. Amen.

PERSEVERANCE

THE STRENGTH TO KEEP GOING
WHEN YOU WANT TO QUIT

"Let us run with endurance the race God has set before us."
~ Hebrews 12:1 (NLT)

The Race That Broke — and Revealed — a Champion

He wasn't supposed to win. Not against the record holders. Not against the polished champions whose names were already etched in Olympic history.

But as Derek Redmond sprinted down the back curve of the 400-meter semifinal in Barcelona, 1992, something tore — not in the track around him, but deep inside his own leg. A sharp, snapping pain sliced through his stride. His hamstring gave way.

The roar of the stadium blurred into silence.

He fell to the ground, clutching his leg, agony and disbelief etched across his face. For a moment the world held its breath. Then the stretchers came — the medical team waving frantically, motioning for him to stay down.

But Derek Redmond didn't stay down.

Through tears, he pushed against the track and lifted himself upright. One step. Then another. He began to hobble forward, refusing the hands that tried to help him off. Refusing to quit.

The crowd, stunned at first, began to rise.

Applause rippled across the stadium as realization spread — he was still moving. He wasn't competing now; he was enduring.

Then something happened that would mark Olympic history forever.

From the stands, a gray-haired man broke through security. Guards reached to stop him, but he waved them aside. Wearing nothing more than a t-shirt, jogging shorts and a father's heart, Jim Redmond sprinted toward his son.

He wrapped an arm around Derek's shoulders, steadying him. The cameras zoomed in. You could see Derek's tears. You could see his father whispering something — words drowned out by the thunder of the crowd.

Together, step by step, they began to walk.

The stadium erupted — an entire world watching not a race, but a revelation.

They didn't run for a medal that day. They walked for something greater: love that refuses to let go.

Derek Redmond didn't finish alone. And that, perhaps, was the truest finish line of all.

Because sometimes perseverance isn't about speed or strength — it's about presence.

Sometimes God's presence doesn't appear in triumph or victory laps.

Sometimes it comes as a Father stepping onto the track, refusing to let His child fall alone.

When the Race Hurts

Life has a way of pulling hamstrings in the middle of dreams.

You start strong — vision clear, energy high — and then something snaps. A door closes. A prayer feels unanswered. A plan collapses under pressure.

The crowd that once cheered you on grows quiet. The track stretches long and lonely. And everything in you whispers, *It's over.*

But perseverance doesn't listen to that voice. Perseverance is the holy defiance that says, Even if I can't run, I will walk. And *even if I can't walk, I will lean on the One who walks with me.*

Hebrews 12:1 says,

> *"Let us run with endurance the race God has set before us." (NLT)*

Notice it doesn't say the race we chose. Sometimes the course winds through valleys you never planned to travel.

Perseverance isn't the absence of pain — it's faith's refusal to surrender to it.

The God Who Steps Onto the Track

When Jim Redmond ran to his son, he broke protocol. Olympic rules didn't allow spectators on the field. But love doesn't wait for permission when compassion is required.

That's the heart of the Father.

When Adam fell, God stepped into the garden.

When Israel groaned in slavery, God stepped into history.

When humanity lay broken, God stepped into flesh.

He didn't shout from the stands — He came down to the track.

Jesus knows the pain of perseverance. He knows what it's like to collapse under the weight of purpose. He stumbled beneath the cross, blood mixing with dust. But even then, Heaven wasn't silent. The Father's plan was still unfolding.

Perseverance doesn't always feel divine — but it's always directed. The Father never leaves you limping alone.

The Middle of the Race

Every believer eventually reaches "the back stretch" — that place between promise and fulfillment where the muscles burn and vision blurs.

It's the wilderness between Egypt and Canaan.

The waiting between anointing and appointment.

The silence between prayer and answer.

The middle is where perseverance matures.

Anyone can start a race. Many can finish if the path is short. But true faith lives in the in-between — in the days that test your resolve and refine your trust.

Derek's father didn't carry him across the line. He simply held him upright. God does the same. He doesn't remove every pain; He redeems it with presence.

Each limp becomes worship. Each step becomes testimony. Each tear becomes seed for joy.

When Perseverance Feels Personal

I've known what it's like to stand in the middle of an unfinished track — to have plans delayed, doors closed, and prayers that seem unanswered.

In those moments, perseverance stopped being a concept and became a choice.

Not the loud kind that clenches fists, but the quiet kind that whispers, God, I trust You anyway.

Sometimes all you can do is keep walking — through the fog, through uncertainty, through exhaustion. Yet those are often the steps Heaven applauds most.

God never asked us to run fast; He asked us to run faithful.

Learning from the Limp

In Genesis 32, Jacob wrestled all night with an angel. He refused to let go until God blessed him. By morning, he limped away — but he also walked in a new identity.

Perseverance will leave you with a limp. But it's a holy limp — a reminder that you've seen God face-to-face and still kept moving.

Your limp is not a loss; it's proof of endurance.

Paul carried his own limp when he wrote,

> *"We are pressed on every side by troubles, but we are not crushed."*
> *~ 2 Corinthians 4:8 (NLT)*

Those who persevere learn to walk with both pain and purpose.

> *"Though sinless, He learned obedience through the things He suffered"*
> *~ Hebrews 5:8 (NLT)*

The Crowd of Witnesses

Hebrews 12:1 (NLT) paints a powerful picture:

> *"Since we are surrounded by such a huge crowd of witnesses... let us run with endurance the race God has set before us."*

You're not running alone. The stands of Heaven are filled with those who finished their laps of faith — Abraham, Sarah, Moses, Ruth, Esther, Paul — all cheering for you to keep going.

And sometimes, the ones who cheer loudest are the people you've inspired along the way without even knowing it.

Your perseverance becomes someone else's permission to believe again.

Finishing with the Father

As Derek Redmond and his father crossed the finish line, the cameras zoomed in on their embrace. No medals. No trophies. Just tears and triumph of another kind.

When you finally cross your finish line — when your faith is tested, refined, and complete — you'll find your Father waiting there too.

He won't greet you with statistics or times. He'll wrap His arms around you and whisper, "Well done, my good and faithful servant. You finished your race."

In that moment, every limp will make sense. Every tear will be redeemed. Every delay will be revealed as divine preparation.

Perseverance was never about the gold — it was always about the glory of finishing with the Father beside you.

Principles for the Journey

Perseverance is the courage to take the next step when everything in you wants to stop.

1. PERSEVERANCE IS PARTNERSHIP

When your strength runs out, perseverance begins where God's presence takes over.

"I will never leave you nor forsake you."
~ Hebrews 13:5 (NLT)

You're not running alone; Heaven runs with you.

2. PERSEVERANCE VALUES PROGRESS OVER PACE

When your strength runs out, perseverance begins where God's presence takes over.

"Be steadfast, immovable, always abounding in the work of the Lord."
~ 1 Corinthians 15:58 (NLT)

God measures faithfulness, not finish times.

3. PERSEVERANCE TURNS LIMPS INTO TESTIMONIES

The places where you struggle most often become the places where God's strength shines brightest.

"My grace is all you need. My power works best in weakness."
~ 2 Corinthians 12:9 (NLT)

The scars of struggle become stories of God's sustaining strength.

4. PERSEVERANCE MATURES THE BELIEVER IN THE MIDDLE

It's in the long stretch between "start" and "finish" that God does His deepest refining work.

"Let perseverance finish its work so that you may be mature and complete."
~ James 1:4 (NLT)

Don't despise the distance — the middle is where endurance is formed.

5. PERSEVERANCE REMEMBERS THE FATHER ALWAYS STEPS IN

When your legs give way, His arms become the strength that carries you forward.

"When you pass through the waters, I will be with you."
~ Isaiah 43:2 (NLT)

When you can't run another step, He will carry you.

Reflect & Apply

1. Where in your life do you feel tempted to stop running?

2. How have you seen the Father "step onto the track" to walk with you in hardship?

3. What does perseverance look like for you in this current season — speed or simply standing?

4. Who might need to witness your endurance to find courage for their own race?

5. What would finishing with the Father, not just for Him, look like in your story?

Prayer

Father, thank you for never leaving me on the track alone. When dreams tear and strength fails, remind me that Your arm is still around me. Teach me to see You not only at the finish line, but in every painful step between. Give me courage to rise after every fall, grace to keep moving when I feel spent, and faith to trust Your pace when mine falters. Let my perseverance become worship — every limp, every tear, every step a declaration that You are enough. In Jesus' name, Amen.

QUIETNESS

STRENGTH IS OFTEN FOUND IN STILLNESS

"This is what the Sovereign Lord says: 'In returning and rest you shall be saved; in quietness and confidence shall be your strength.'"
~ Isaiah 30:15 (NLT)

The Teacher in the Mist

The mist rolled low over Lake Lucerne, curling like breath from the earth as dawn broke over the Swiss hills. The air was sharp with mountain cold, but from a small cottage on the slope came the sound of life — young voices reciting letters, the scrape of a hand plane against cedar, the occasional burst of laughter that made even the weary smile.

An old man stepped into the light — stooped, steady, his hands marked by both work and weather. Johann Heinrich Pestalozzi had once walked in the company of kings and scholars. His name had echoed in the academies of Europe; his vision for education had reshaped nations. But now, in his final years, the crowds were gone. His schools had closed. His reputation had faded into quiet memory.

What remained were a few orphaned children, a patch of earth to till, and a workshop scarred by decades of use.

To some, this looked like failure — a great man reduced to obscurity. But those who visited Seelisberg would leave changed. They would see wisdom carved deep into the lines of his face, hear the gentleness in his instruction, and sense that this quiet life was not an ending, but a homecoming.

Each morning, Pestalozzi prayed — not for prominence, but for faithfulness.

He taught his small flock of children to read, to mend roofs, to hoe garden rows, and to give thanks for bread and for rain. He spoke of God's delight in honest work, of dignity found in service, and of how greatness begins in humility.

He never built an empire. He built a life anchored in peace.

When he died, they buried him near the little workshop, where the sound of children's laughter still drifted through the hills.

He left behind no fortune, no monuments — only the quiet proof that true strength is found not in acclaim, but in alignment with God's heart.

His life whispered the words of Scripture:

> *"Make it your ambition to lead a quiet life, to mind your own affairs, and to work with your hands... so that your daily life may win the respect of outsiders."*
> *~ 1 Thessalonians 4:11-12 (NLT)*

THE GIFT OF STILLNESS

Quietness is not the absence of sound — it's the presence of peace. It's the place where the soul stops striving long enough to hear the voice of God.

The world celebrates motion: faster, louder, more visible. But Heaven honors stillness — that sacred rhythm where faith learns to rest without retreating.

When Elijah stood on Mount Horeb, battered by wind, earthquake, and fire, God wasn't in any of it. Then came a whisper — gentle, almost imperceptible — and Elijah covered his face. 1 Kings 19:11-13 (NLT)

The voice of God is often found not in the noise of urgency, but in the quiet of surrender.

Our culture equates silence with weakness, but Scripture says otherwise.

> *"In quietness and confidence shall be your strength."*
> *~ Isaiah 30:15 (NLT)*

Quietness is not passivity; it's power under control. It's faith that no longer needs to prove itself because it trusts Who holds tomorrow.

Jesus and the Sacred Pause

Even Jesus practiced stillness.

Throughout the Gospels, He often withdrew from the crowds — not because He was weary of people, but because He longed for the Father's presence.

Before every miracle, every message, every major decision, He found a mountain or a quiet place to pray.

In Mark 1:35 (NLT) we read:

> *"Before daybreak the next morning, Jesus got up and went out to an isolated place to pray."*

He healed multitudes, yet often told people not to speak of it. He entered cities in silence. He chose solitude over spectacle.

And in that quiet rhythm between doing and being, He revealed a truth that still confronts us today: you can't hear Heaven while drowning in noise.

The strength of Jesus' ministry wasn't in the crowds; it was in His communion.

He showed us that quietness is not withdrawal — it's recalibration.

When Quiet Feels Uncomfortable

Stillness can be unsettling at first.

When the noise fades, you start to hear the thoughts and fears you've buried under busyness. The silence becomes a mirror — showing what activity used to hide.

But that's where transformation begins.

God's peace doesn't fill noisy hearts; it fills surrendered ones.

Psalm 46:10 (NLT) says,

> *"Be still, and know that I am God."*

Those two verbs are inseparable — be still and know.

We cannot know His nearness until we stop long enough to sense it.

Quietness is the soil where revelation grows.

The Strength Beneath the Surface

Stillness doesn't mean stagnation.

A river looks calm on the surface but carries immense power beneath.

Likewise, a believer anchored in God's peace moves steadily, not frantically. They know the difference between motion and momentum — between activity and anointing.

Isaiah 32:17 (NLT) says,

> *"And this righteousness will bring peace. Yes, it will bring quietness and confidence forever."*

That's the paradox of faith: the deeper your roots of quietness, the greater your reach of strength.

Pestalozzi's final years were not a retreat from life; they were a return to what mattered. In the slowing down, he became more fruitful — not in fame, but in faithfulness.

He didn't build schools; he built souls.

He didn't chase applause; he cultivated peace.

And in Heaven's record book, that's what endures.

Quiet Strength in the Noise of Life

There's a quiet strength that comes when you stop defending yourself, stop over explaining, stop rushing to fix everything that's out of your control.

When you entrust your reputation to God.

When you stop reacting and start resting.

When you realize silence can sometimes preach louder than speech.

Moses learned this when the Israelites panicked at the Red Sea.

He told them,

> *"The Lord will fight for you; you need only to be still."*
> *~ Exodus 14:14 (NLT)*

Stillness didn't mean doing nothing — it meant trusting everything.

And in that moment, God moved the sea.

Quietness is not weakness — it's warfare done in confidence, not chaos.

Learning to Dwell in the Slow Lane

We live in an age that confuses hurry with purpose.

Even in ministry, we can mistake motion for progress. But Jesus never rushed. He walked everywhere He went. Even when the need was urgent, He moved at the pace of peace.

When Lazarus died, Jesus delayed His arrival — not out of indifference, but divine timing. In the pause, God prepared resurrection.

The same is true for us. God often works most deeply when He seems most silent.

Our job isn't to force the outcome; it's to stay faithful in the quiet middle.

Principles for the Journey

Quietness is the strength that rises when you stop striving long enough to let God speak.

1. QUIETNESS IS NOT ABSENCE; IT'S AWARENESS

In the pause between your thoughts, God often reveals the things your busyness kept you from seeing.

"Be still and know that I am God."
~ Psalm 46:10 (NLT)

Stillness opens your heart to see what activity can't.

2. QUIETNESS RESTORES PERSPECTIVE

When life feels loud, quietness pulls you back to the place where God's peace resets what your fears distorted.

"He leads me beside peaceful streams; He renews my strength."
~ Psalm 23:2-3 (NLT)

Peace isn't found in escape — it's found in presence.

3. QUIETNESS BECOMES THE LOUDEST FORM OF TRUST

Sometimes the strongest statement of faith is choosing stillness when everything in you wants to act.

"The Lord will fight for you; you need only to be still."
~ Exodus 14:14 (NLT)

Let God defend what only He can sustain.

4. QUIETNESS PREPARES THE HEART FOR REVELATION

When the noise around you fades, the whisper of God rises with a clarity busyness can never produce.

"After the fire came a gentle whisper."
~ 1 Kings 19:12 (NLT)

God often speaks clearest when everything else is quiet.

5. QUIETNESS IS STRENGTH DISGUISED AS STILLNESS

Real strength isn't always seen in motion — it's often found in the calm resolve of a heart anchored in God.

"In quietness and confidence shall be your strength."
~ Isaiah 30:15 (NLT)

The peace of God is not passive — it's powerful.

Reflect & Apply

1. When was the last time you truly stopped to rest in God's presence?

2. What "noise" in your life makes it difficult to hear His voice?

3. How could stillness become a regular rhythm of your day rather than a rare retreat?

4. What might God be trying to teach you in this season of quiet or delay?

5. How can your calm spirit bring peace into the environments you influence?

Father, teach me to find strength in stillness. Quiet my anxious thoughts and steady my restless spirit. When the world demands noise and motion, help me remember that Your voice often comes as a whisper. Lead me beside peaceful waters until Your rhythm becomes my own. May my life echo the truth that peace is not the absence of struggle but the presence of trust. And in the silence of surrender, let me hear You say again, "Be still, and know that I am God." Amen.

RESTORATION

WHEN GOD REBUILDS
WHAT LIFE HAS BROKEN

"They will rebuild the ancient ruins and restore the places long devastated."
~ Isaiah 61:4 (NLT)

The Church That Rose from the Ashes

The winter wind swept through Dresden like a ghost — a whisper of all that once was. Rubble still marked the old quarter, blackened stone and twisted steel where music and laughter had once filled the air.

For decades, the people of Dresden walked past the same pile of ruins — the charred bones of the great Frauenkirche (FROW-en-keer-kuh), the Church of Our Lady. Its dome, once the crown of the city's skyline, lay collapsed in a heap of soot and silence.

In 1945, fire had fallen from the heavens. Allied bombers turned the night sky into an inferno. The proud Baroque cathedral that had stood for two centuries was reduced to a monument of loss. Locals called it simply *die Ruine* — "the ruin."

Year after year it remained untouched — a scar of stone left as a warning, and a wound that refused to heal.

But after the Iron Curtain fell and Germany was reunited, something remarkable began. Ordinary people — bricklayers, widows, students, engineers — returned to the ruins with purpose in their hands and hope in their hearts.

They refused to forget. They refused to move on.

Instead, they began to rebuild.

Every fallen stone was lifted, cleaned, and numbered. Old maps and photographs guided the craftsmen as they pieced the structure together like a puzzle of grace. Blackened stones from the fire were set beside new white ones, their contrast deliberate — a confession and a promise.

For eleven years they worked, quietly, faithfully, until in 2005 the dome rose again.

When the bells rang for the first time in sixty years, the people of Dresden wept openly in the streets — not for what had been destroyed, but for what had been restored.

Sunlight poured through the stained-glass windows onto the very floor where ashes had once fallen. The scars remained, each dark stone a memorial of pain, but also a declaration of redemption.

The Frauenkirche was no longer a ruin.

It was resurrection in stone.

God's Blueprint for Broken Things

The story of Dresden mirrors the story of the human heart.

Every one of us has places bombed by disappointment, walls cracked by betrayal, and foundations shaken by loss.

Life's fire doesn't always burn buildings — sometimes it burns dreams.

But just as those German craftsmen refused to discard a single stone, God refuses to discard the pieces of your life. He is the Master Builder who specializes in reconstruction.

Psalm 147:3 (NLT) says,

> *"He heals the brokenhearted and bandages their wounds."*

He doesn't sweep away the rubble; He redeems it.

When Isaiah 61 speaks of "rebuilding the ancient ruins," it's not about architecture — it's about people. About lives once shattered by sin, restored by grace. About souls that once echoed with emptiness, now ringing with praise.

Restoration is not cosmetic. It's covenantal.

It's God taking what the enemy meant for destruction and using it as the foundation for something stronger.

When the Fire Has Fallen

Everyone faces seasons when everything collapses.

It might be a marriage that faltered, a dream that died, a reputation that burned in misunderstanding.

When that happens, it's easy to believe the story is over.

But resurrection always begins in ruins.

The cross looked like finality, yet three days later, the stone rolled away.

The disciples' faith looked like ashes, but Pentecost lit it again with holy fire.

God never wastes pain. What feels like destruction can become the excavation of destiny.

If you look closely at the rebuilt Frauenkirche, the dark stones are still visible, forming patterns across the façade. The architects intentionally left them that way — visible reminders of both the tragedy and the triumph.

That's how grace works. It doesn't erase the fire; it redeems it.

Your scars become the very proof of His mercy.

The Work of Restoration

Restoration takes time.

Eleven years to rebuild a church.

A lifetime to rebuild a heart.

It begins when we hand God the fragments and trust Him to know where each piece belongs.

Some stones must be turned over. Some must be cleaned. Some must be set aside until the foundation is ready. But in His timing, every fragment finds its place.

Philippians 1:6 (NLT) declares,

> *"He who began the good work within you will continue His work until it is finally finished."*

God doesn't leave projects half-done.

He's not discouraged by your delays or disqualifications.

What He starts, He finishes — even if He has to rebuild you brick by brick.

When God Restores, He Renews

Restoration isn't just about putting back what was lost; it's about revealing what's new.

Job 42:10 (NLT) says,

> *"When Job prayed for his friends, the Lord restored his fortunes. In fact, the Lord gave him twice as much as before."*

Job's story didn't end in ruins; it ended in renewal.

The same God who allowed the test wrote the turnaround.

When God restores, He doesn't return you to what you were; He transforms you into who you were meant to be.

He weaves light through darkness, hope through heartbreak, and grace through grief until your life becomes a mosaic of mercy.

The Beauty of Scars

Some believers hide their scars, ashamed of the smoke that still lingers from old fires. But scars are sacred — they tell the story of survival.

Even Jesus kept His.

After the resurrection, He could have erased the nail marks, yet He chose to show them.

> *"Put your finger here," He told Thomas.*
> *~ John 20:27 (NLT)*

Why? Because redemption is never ashamed of its past; it redeems it.

Like the dark stones in Dresden's walls, your scars don't ruin your beauty — they complete it. They testify that grace is real and healing is possible.

Rebuilding Together

Notice that Dresden wasn't rebuilt by one architect alone. It took a community — masons, artists, volunteers, and donors from around the world.

Restoration is rarely a solo project.

God uses people to help lift the stones we cannot lift alone.

Galatians 6:2 (NLT) says,

> *"Share each other's burdens, and in this way obey the law of Christ."*

You are both a construction site and a craftsman. God restores you so that you, in turn, can help restore others.

The Sound of the Bell

When the Frauenkirche bell rang again after sixty years, its tone carried something deeper than music. It was forgiveness turned into sound.

That's what restoration does — it rings hope into places long silent.

It declares, *"The fire is over, but the story isn't."*

Your bell will ring again too.

One day, joy will echo where sorrow used to live.

Peace will replace panic. Praise will fill the places where pain once spoke loudest.

Because the God who rebuilds ruins is still at work — in cities, in families, in you.

Principles for the Journey

Restoration is the miracle where God lifts what life has shattered and rebuilds it with a beauty only His hands can make.

1. RESTORATION REBUILDS WHAT WAS BROKEN

With God, ruins aren't the end of the story — they're the starting place where mercy begins to rise.

"They will rebuild the ancient ruins."
~ Isaiah 61:4 (NLT)

God doesn't discard the broken pieces; He fits them back together with purpose.

2. RESTORATION HONORS YOUR SCARS, NOT HIDES THEM

What the world calls damage, God calls testimony — evidence of the grace that held you together.

"My grace is sufficient for you."
~ 2 Corinthians 12:9 (NLT)

Your dark stones are not shame — they're testimony.

3. RESTORATION REQUIRES PATIENCE WITH GOD'S TIMING

Some rebuilding happens stone by stone, in seasons where it seems like nothing is changing — but Heaven is still at work.

"Let perseverance finish its work."
~ James 1:4 (NLT)

God builds carefully so that what rises will stand.

4. **RESTORATION STRENGTHENS COMMUNITY AND INVITES HELP**

   God often restores us through the hands of others — the ones who help lift the pieces we can't carry alone.

   "Share each other's burdens."
   ~ Galatians 6:2 (NLT)

   Healing accelerates when we rebuild together, not alone.

5. **RESTORATION ENDS IN GREATER GLORY THAN WHAT WAS LOST**

   When God restores, He doesn't simply return what was taken — He rebuilds with a glory that makes the old seem small.

   "The glory of this latter house shall be greater than the former."
   ~ Haggai 2:9 (KJV)

   God never restores to what you were — He restores to more than you imagined.

Reflect & Apply

1. What part of your life feels like rubble right now?

2. How have you seen God rebuild what once seemed beyond repair?

3. What "dark stones" in your story could become testimonies of grace?

4. Who has God placed around you to help in your rebuilding process?

5. How can you become part of someone else's restoration story?

Father, thank you that no ruin is beyond Your reach. Where fire has fallen in my life, rebuild with grace. Pick up the stones I've abandoned, and set them again in Your perfect design. Teach me to see beauty in the burn marks, and faith in the waiting. When others only see rubble, help me to see resurrection. May my life become a cathedral of Your mercy — a place where Your light pours through the cracks and Your glory rings like a bell of hope. Amen.

SELF-CONTROL

MASTER YOUR IMPULSES
THEY DON'T HAVE TO MASTER YOU

"Better a patient person than a warrior, one with self-control than one who takes a city."
~ Proverbs 16:32 (NLT)

Tea with the Enemy

It was 1994, and South Africa stood on the edge of an abyss. Decades of apartheid had carved wounds so deep that peace seemed impossible. The world watched as a nation simmered with anger — long-suppressed rage now rising like steam from a volcano.

In the presidential office of Pretoria, Nelson Mandela stood by the window, gazing out over a city divided not just by color but by history.

He was now the elected leader of a nation that had once imprisoned him for twenty-seven years. The irony was not lost on him — nor was the weight of it.

Outside, soldiers still patrolled the streets. Inside, his advisors argued.

"Now is the time to make them pay," some urged. "Justice must be felt."

Mandela turned from the window, his face calm, his tone quiet enough to still the room.

"No," he said. "We must show them something greater than justice. We must show them mercy."

That evening he invited his former prison guards — white Afrikaners — to join him for tea.

Cameras flashed as he poured for them himself, steady hands betraying none of the emotion that must have roared inside.

He smiled, spoke gently, and listened more than he spoke.

In that act he did what few leaders could do — he conquered the anger that had every right to consume him.

He chose the rare strength of self-control in the face of rightful revenge.

Months later, at his inauguration, one of the very men who had once stood watch over him in prison sat among the honored guests.

Mandela lifted his hand to the crowd and spoke not of vengeance but of forgiveness — not of retaliation but rebuilding.

The world saw a political miracle. Heaven saw something deeper — a man who mastered his impulses and set a nation free.

He could have broken his enemies. Instead, he rebuilt a country.

Power Under Control

Self-control isn't the absence of emotion; it's the rule of the Spirit over emotion.

It's not coldness — it's clarity.

It doesn't erase feeling; it redeems it.

Proverbs 25:28 (NLT) warns,

> *"A person without self-control is like a city with broken-down walls."*

Mandela's life proved the reverse: a person with self-control becomes a fortified city where peace can dwell.

When you master your impulses, you don't lose power — you gain authority.

You become dangerous in the right way: a person whose strength can build instead of burn.

Jesus and the Sacred Restraint

Mandela's mercy mirrored a greater example. When Jesus stood before Pilate, He too had the power to destroy His enemies with a word — yet He remained silent.

> *"He did not retaliate when He was insulted, nor threaten revenge when He suffered. He left His case in the hands of God."*
> *~ 1 Peter 2:23 (NLT)*

Self-control is Christ-control — the Spirit governing your responses when your rights are screaming for revenge.

The world calls that weakness. Heaven calls it strength.

The War Within

Most battles of self-control don't happen in parliament chambers but in private moments — in the car when you've been cut off, in the office when you're misunderstood, in the home when a careless word stings.

The enemy loves to turn temporary anger into permanent damage.

But every time you pause before you pounce, you build a wall that protects your peace.

Nehemiah rebuilt Jerusalem's walls stone by stone under constant threat. Likewise, self-control is constructed moment by moment, choice by choice.

You rebuild your inner Jerusalem every time you say, "Lord, guard my heart — don't let me react out of hurt."

When You Have the Right to React

There will be moments when you could strike back and be justified — when forgiveness feels like surrender and silence feels like defeat.

That's where the Spirit whispers: *Strength isn't proving you're right; it's staying righteous.*

Self-control is a holy refusal to let pain dictate purpose.

It says, "I will not let my past decide my response."

Mandela understood that anger could unify for a moment but destroy for a generation.

So he chose the long road of restraint.

He didn't deny the wound — he disarmed it.

That's what the Holy Spirit does in us. He doesn't erase memory; He redeems reaction.

Walls and Gates

If self-control is a city, then its walls are boundaries and its gates are choices.

You decide what gets in — what thoughts, voices, and habits are allowed to enter.

A wall without gates is legalism; gates without walls are chaos.

God calls you to build both — strength with structure, grace with guardrails.

Proverbs 16:32 (NLT) isn't about temper alone; it's about governance.

The strongest kingdom you'll ever rule is your own spirit.

The Spirit's Partnership

You can't grit your way to self-control.

It is the final fruit of the Spirit because it grows only in a Spirit-filled life.

Galatians 5:22-23 (NLT) lists it last not because it's least, but because it's the seal that holds the others together.

Love needs self-control to stay pure.

Joy needs self-control to stay consistent.

Peace needs self-control to stay protected.

When the Spirit governs your heart, your emotions serve your purpose instead of sabotaging it.

Lessons from a Prison Cell

For twenty-seven years Mandela lived behind bars — years that could have bred bitterness.

Yet those years became the forge of his temperament. Prison didn't just confine him; it refined him.

He learned to listen before speaking, to think before acting, to plan before provoking.

The bars that once held him became the discipline that later held a nation together.

Self-control isn't born in comfort; it's forged in constraint.

When God allows limitations, He's training your will and toughening your trust.

A Kingdom of Calm

In a world that equates volume with power, the Spirit-led life is a kingdom of calm.

You don't have to shout to be strong or react to be relevant.

Quiet control confuses the enemy.

He expects explosion and finds peace instead.

Romans 12:21 (NLT) says,

> *"Don't let evil conquer you, but conquer evil by doing good."*

That's the Mandela method — and the Christ model.

Overcome not by outburst but by out-love.

Principles for the Journey

Self-control is the disciplined strength that conquers battles inside you long before they ever reach the world around you.

1. SELF-CONTROL IS SPIRIT-CONTROL

The strongest victories are won when the Spirit leads your responses instead of your impulses.

"Let the Holy Spirit guide your lives."
~ Galatians 5:16 (NLT)

The goal isn't willpower but surrendered power.

2. SELF-CONTROL CHOOSES RESTRAINT OVER REVENGE

Real power is revealed not by how fiercely you can strike, but by how faithfully you can stay your hand.

"Better a patient person than a warrior."
~ Proverbs 16:32 (NLT)

Mercy doesn't weaken justice; it redeems it.

3. SELF-CONTROL BUILDS BOUNDARIES THAT PROTECT BLESSING

Every boundary you build becomes a gatekeeper for the peace God is trying to preserve in you.

"A person without self-control is like a city with broken-down walls."
~ Proverbs 25:28 (NLT)

Guard your peace as carefully as you guard your purpose.

4. SELF-CONTROL TRUSTS GOD'S TIMING IN THE WAITING

When you refuse to rush ahead of God, patience becomes the place where your strength is renewed.

"Those who trust in the Lord will find new strength."
~ Isaiah 40:31 (NLT)

Delay is not defeat — it's divine preparation.

5. SELF-CONTROL GROWS AS THE SPIRIT PRODUCES FREEDOM

The more you yield to God's leading, the more your life sheds the chains of old reactions and steps into real freedom.

"Where the Spirit of the Lord is, there is freedom."
~ 2 Corinthians 3:17 (NLT)

The more you submit to God's governance, the freer your life becomes.

Reflect & Apply

1. Where in your life do emotions most often override wisdom?

2. What would "pouring tea for your enemies" look like in your world right now?

3. Which boundaries or disciplines help you stay Spirit-led when provoked?

4. How can restraint become a witness to those around you?

5. What past limitation or "prison season" has taught you holy restraint?

Father, thank you for the Spirit who gives power over my impulses. When anger rises or fear demands a reaction, teach me to pause and listen. Help me respond with wisdom instead of emotion, with mercy instead of vengeance. Let Your peace rule my heart like walls around a city rebuilt by grace. And when I have the right to retaliate, remind me that Jesus chose a cross over a crown so that I could choose restraint over ruin. Amen.

TRUST

RESTING WHEN YOU DON'T UNDERSTAND

"Trust in the Lord with all your heart; do not depend on your own understanding."
~ Proverbs 3:5 (NLT)

The Shore of Questions

The horizon over the English Channel was gray that morning — a soft, endless kind of gray that blurred sea and sky until they became one. Corrie ten Boom stood at the edge of a quiet shore years after the war, hands folded in front of her, coat buttoned against the wind. The tide whispered at her feet — the same sea that had once separated her from her family, from freedom, from understanding.

The wind carried the smell of salt and memory. Every wave seemed to echo a prayer that had gone unanswered.

During the war, she had begged Heaven for rescue that didn't come, for mercy that seemed to bounce off prison walls.

In Ravensbrück concentration camp, she had watched her sister Betsie grow thinner by the day, her faith somehow growing stronger even as her body failed.

Corrie couldn't understand it — how peace could exist in a place built for suffering.

One night, as frost crept through the barracks, Betsie's whisper cut through the dark:

"Tell them — there is no pit so deep that He is not deeper still."

Those were her last words.

After liberation, Corrie tried to make sense of it all — the years of loss, the silence, the questions that refused answers.

She traveled, she spoke, she forgave — but sometimes at night, when the applause faded, she still wondered why God had allowed such pain.

Why the waiting?

Why the waste?

Why the silence that sounded like abandonment?

Now, decades later, standing before the same sea that had once divided her from hope, she realized she was still learning the same lesson: **trust is not understanding — it's resting when understanding won't come.**

The Ticket and the Train

She remembered her father's story — a memory as gentle as the wind that brushed her face.

As a child she had feared death, terrified at the thought of losing him.

He had smiled, brushing a strand of hair from her eyes.

"Corrie," he'd said, "when we go on a journey by train, when do I give you your ticket?"

"Just before we get on," she'd whispered.

"Exactly. And our wise Father in heaven knows when you're going to need things too. Don't run ahead of Him."

The memory warmed her like sunlight through cloud.

That was trust — receiving grace at the moment it's needed, not a moment before.

She gazed at the water and understood: her life had always been held by hands unseen, timed by a wisdom unhurried.

Trust doesn't ask for the whole map — just the next step.

It is faith that has learned to exhale.

Faith Begins, Trust Endures

Faith is the spark that believes; trust is the steady flame that keeps burning when the wind howls.

Faith steps onto the waves; trust stays when the storm doesn't stop.

Faith says, "God will make a way."

Trust says, "Even if He doesn't, He's still good."

Corrie had prayed for freedom — and instead, God gave endurance.

She had asked for deliverance — and instead, He gave depth.

In the prison of circumstance, He had taught her the freedom of surrender.

Now she saw: the silence of God had been the sound of His patience — a Father waiting until she was ready to receive what He was ready to give.

The Long Middle

Every believer knows the middle ground — the space between promise and fulfillment, prayer and answer.

It's the wilderness between Egypt and Canaan, the stretch of silence where faith is refined into trust.

Faith begins with declaration: *I believe!*

Trust continues with determination: *I still believe.*

In the long middle, God teaches us to release control.

He hides His hand to reveal His heart.

Job learned it when he said,

> *"Though He slay me, yet will I trust Him."*
> *~Job 13:15 (NLT)*

Mary learned it when she whispered, *"Be it unto me according to Your word."*

Jesus embodied it when He prayed, *"Not My will, but Yours be done."*

Trust is faith after the shouting stops.

It's the calm that remains when answers don't.

The Mystery of God's Timing

The sea before Corrie shimmered faintly, the color of pewter.

She thought of all the times she had tried to run ahead of God — to make sense of what He hadn't yet explained.

But His timing had always proven perfect in hindsight.

The fleas in the barracks — those miserable pests she once cursed — had kept the guards away, allowing them to read Scripture aloud without fear.

Even suffering had served purpose.

God's providence isn't always pretty up close.

It's like embroidery: the knots and tangles on the underside look chaotic, but flip it over, and the pattern is revealed.

Trust is living on the underside of that embroidery and still believing the Artist knows what He's doing.

When Understanding Isn't Coming

We crave explanations.

We want closure, clarity, control.

But God often offers something better — **companionship**.

In every unanswered prayer, His presence stays constant.

In every delay, His goodness remains.

Isaiah 26:3 (NLT) promises,

> *"You will keep in perfect peace all who trust in You, all whose thoughts are fixed on You."*

Peace doesn't come from knowing why.

It comes from knowing *Who*.

Corrie opened her eyes to the horizon and smiled faintly.

She didn't need the full picture anymore.

The fragments were enough, because she knew the Painter.

Trust When You Can't See the Finish Line

Life rarely gives us straight roads. Most days feel more like the Channel that morning — fog over water, no clear line between here and there.

Trust is what keeps the soul steady in the gray.

It's what whispers, *"He's still leading,"* when sight fails and senses falter.

Psalm 37:5 (NLT) says,

> *"Commit everything you do to the Lord. Trust Him, and He will help you."*

That word commit means to roll it onto Him — to place the full weight of your uncertainty on His shoulders.

You don't have to see the finish line to finish well.

You just have to keep walking in the direction of His voice.

Principles for the Journey

Trust is the bridge your soul crosses when sight stops and faith takes the lead.

1. TRUST IS MATURED FAITH

Trust is what faith becomes when it stops striving and starts settling into God's strength.

"Be still, and know that I am God."
~ Psalm 46:10 (NLT)

Faith believes; trust rests.

2. TRUST REMEMBERS THAT GOD'S SILENCE IS NOT HIS ABSENCE

In the hush between prayers and answers, God is often doing His deepest work.

"I will never leave you nor forsake you."
~ Hebrews 13:5 (NLT)

Heaven's quiet often hides Heaven's work.

3. TRUST RECEIVES GRACE RIGHT ON TIME

God's provision may not come early, but it never arrives late — not by a single breath.

"Let us come boldly to the throne of our gracious God. There we will receive His mercy, and we will find grace to help us when we need it most."
~ Hebrews 4:16 (NLT)

The ticket is given just before the train departs.

4. TRUST SURRENDERS EVEN WITHOUT UNDERSTANDING

When certainty fades, trust steps forward — anchored not in answers but in the One who holds them.

"Lean not on your own understanding."
~ Proverbs 3:5 (NLT)

You don't have to know the plan to trust the Planner.

5. TRUST GROWS PEACE IN THE WAITING

The longer you wait with God, the deeper your roots of peace grow beneath the surface.

"Those who trust in the Lord will find new strength."
~ Isaiah 40:31 (NLT)

Waiting isn't wasted; it's worship in slow motion.

Reflect & Apply

1. What situation in your life feels like the "gray horizon" — unclear, unresolved, uncertain?

2. How has God's timing in past seasons proven wiser than your own plans?

3. Where might you be demanding understanding when God is offering peace?

4. What could it look like to "wait well" — to turn patience into worship?

5. Who in your life needs to see what trusting God looks like in real time?

Father, teach me to trust You when I can't trace You. When Your silence feels heavy and answers seem far away, remind me that You are still near. Help me to rest in Your timing instead of rushing into mine. Give me faith that moves mountains — and trust that stands still when the mountain doesn't move. Teach me the art of resting in the gray, knowing Your grace always arrives right on time. In Jesus' name, Amen.

UNDERSTANDING

WHEN CLARITY COMES THROUGH SURRENDER

"The Lord says, 'I will guide you along the best pathway for your life. I will advise you and watch over you.
~ Psalm 32:8 (NLT)

The year was 1941, and London burned. Night after night, the air raid sirens wailed across the city as families rushed into underground stations — holding blankets, children, and each other — while German bombs thundered overhead. Firestorms lit the sky a hellish orange, casting trembling shadows on the cobblestone streets.

Far from the roar of the front lines, in a dimly lit ambulance depot, a young volunteer named **C. S. Lewis** slipped on his heavy coat and stepped into the smoke-filled night. He was a scholar by training, a thinker shaped by logic, philosophy, and argument. He once believed everything could be explained if you traced the reasoning back far enough. But war has a way of shattering tidy explanations.

Tonight was one of those nights.

As an ambulance driver, Lewis spent his hours pulling wounded men and women from the rubble — holding hands that would not hold on much longer, listening to last words whispered through the dust. Every shift forced him to face questions that philosophy could not quiet.

Why this suffering?

Why so much darkness?

Where was God in all of this?

One night, after hours of navigating collapsing buildings and smoke-blackened alleyways, Lewis found himself walking alone through a quiet street where the fires had mostly died out. Ash drifted like gray snow around a ruined church. The stone walls still stood, but the roof had collapsed inward, and charred beams lay scattered across the pews.

Yet something caught his eye.

A fragment of **stained glass**, still clinging stubbornly to its frame. The window was shattered — only jagged pieces remained — but behind it, the glow of nearby burning buildings shone through, sending fractured rays of red, gold, and blue dancing across the rubble.

Lewis stopped.

The glass was broken. The image incomplete. The story it once depicted — lost. Yet the **light** still poured through it.

And suddenly, that battered fragment became a teacher.

Understanding, he realized, does not always come from seeing the full picture. Sometimes it comes from recognizing that God can shine through what remains — even when the window is shattered.

For years, Lewis had sought answers to suffering: explanations, arguments, coherent justifications for a world in pain. But in that moment, he began to see something deeper.

Understanding is not being able to explain God.

Understanding is recognizing God is present even when explanations fail.

He once believed that to trust God he needed to understand Him. Now he saw the reverse was true: to understand anything at all, he first needed to trust.

Understanding was not clarity of the mind — it was surrender of the heart.

Later, Lewis would write words that grew out of nights like that:

"I do not see everything clearly, but I know that God is good."

It wasn't an answer. It was an anchor.

He surrendered his need for perfect clarity, and in doing so, found the peace his intellect had never achieved.

When the Window Is Broken

We often treat understanding as something God owes us:

"Why did this happen?"

"What are You doing?"

"When will You fix this?"

But Scripture rarely promises explanations. Instead, it offers **presence**.

"Lean not on your own understanding," Proverbs says — not because God wants us ignorant, but because understanding built on our limited perspective will always crumble under the weight of reality.

Real understanding comes when we bring our shattered windows to God and let His light shine through the pieces.

Sometimes clarity doesn't come from answers, but from awareness:

God is here.

God is working.

God is good.

Even here.

Even now.

When God's Light Shines Through Broken Places

Understanding is not the same as information.

It's not the same as certainty.

It's not the same as control.

Understanding is **insight shaped by surrender** — a way of seeing God in the fragments that once confused us.

Some of the deepest understanding in your life may come:

- not when prayers are answered, but when you decide to trust while they aren't
- not when you feel strong, but when you admit you're weak
- not when the situation improves, but when you realize God has been with you the whole time
- not when life stabilizes, but when you stop trying to stabilize it on your own

We gain understanding the same way Lewis did — by seeing God's light shine through what we once thought was ruined.

Principles for the Journey

Understanding begins where striving ends — at the place where God's light breaks through what we can't explain.

1. UNDERSTANDING BEGINS WITH SURRENDER

Clarity comes when the heart finally stops running long enough to hear the whisper of God.

"Be still, and know that I am God."
~ Psalm 46:10 (NLT)

Stillness creates space for God to reveal what rushing never will.

2. UNDERSTANDING COMES IN GOD'S TIMING, NOT OURS

What feels like delay to us is often divine preparation disguised in silence.

"His understanding is beyond comprehension."
~ Isaiah 40:28 (NLT)

We are not waiting for information; we are learning dependence.

3. UNDERSTANDING GROWS WHEN WE RELEASE OUR DEMAND FOR EXPLANATIONS

Sometimes God removes the need to see so we can finally learn to trust.

"We walk by faith, not by sight."
~ 2 Corinthians 5:7 (NLT)

Sometimes sight blinds us; faith clarifies us.

4. UNDERSTANDING IS OFTEN CLEAREST THROUGH BROKEN PLACES

Your most painful moments can become the lenses through which God brings clarity.

"The light shines in the darkness, and the darkness can never extinguish it."
~ John 1:5 (NLT)

God's light shines most vividly through the fractures we try to hide.

5. UNDERSTANDING IS REVEALED, NOT ACHIEVED

Revelation doesn't rise from striving; it comes when your heart finally grows quiet enough to receive it.

"If any of you lacks wisdom, ask God ... and it will be given to you."
~ James 1:5 (NLT)

God reveals truth to the surrendered, not the self-sufficient.

Reflect & Apply

1. What situation in your life are you trying too hard to understand instead of surrendering?

2. Where have you seen God's light shine through something broken?

3. What would it look like to trust God without needing all the answers?

4. Have you mistaken information for understanding? How is God shifting your perspective?

5. What is one area where you need to say, "Lord, I don't understand — but I trust You"?

Prayer

Lord, teach me to trust You even when I do not understand. Shine Your light through the broken places of my life until I see with Your eyes instead of my own. Give me a surrendered heart, a quiet spirit, and a faith that rests in Your goodness. Let Your presence become my understanding. Amen.

VISION

SEEING WHAT GOD SEES BEFORE IT HAPPENS

"Where there is no vision, the people perish."
~ Proverbs 29:18 (KJV)

"Faith is the assurance of things hoped for, the conviction of things not seen."
~ Hebrews 11:1 (ESV)

The Alabama sun hung heavy over Montgomery in 1955. The air was thick with tension — the kind of quiet before a storm when history is about to turn a page. In a modest kitchen on South

Jackson Street, a young pastor sat alone at his table, head bowed, a cup of coffee growing cold beside him.

He was only **twenty-six**.

His name — **Martin Luther King Jr**.

For weeks, the threats had intensified. Anonymous phone calls. Letters filled with venom. A cross burned in his yard. Police protection was inconsistent at best. His wife, Coretta, and their infant daughter were asleep in the next room when the phone rang again.

King lifted the receiver.

A voice hissed, low and violent: **"Listen, preacher. This is your last warning. Get out of town — or we'll blow up your house."**

He hung up slowly. The room felt smaller, the shadows deeper, the air heavier. His hands trembled as he stared at the dark window. The weight of the movement — the protests, the boycotts, the dangers, the hopes of thousands pressed onto his shoulders like a crushing mountain.

He was exhausted.

He was afraid.

And for the first time, he did not know what to do.

He slid the coffee aside, folded his hands, and whispered the prayer that rose from the deepest part of him:

"Lord ... I am weak now. I am faltering. I am losing courage.

I cannot face this alone."

What happened next would mark him for the rest of his life.

In the stillness of that early morning kitchen, a presence filled the room — not loud, not dramatic, but unmistakably real. Later, King would describe it as the voice of Jesus whispering within him:

"Stand up for righteousness. Stand up for truth.

And lo, I will be with you ... even unto the end of the world."

The fear didn't disappear, but something greater took its place.

Vision.

Not the kind that sees with natural eyes, but the kind that is born in the soul — the kind that allows a person to see beyond danger, beyond opposition, beyond the present moment. In that dim kitchen, King saw something more: a nation healed, a people standing together, a world changed.

Not because circumstances were favorable.

Not because the danger disappeared.

But because God revealed a future only faith could see.

Years later, on the steps of the Lincoln Memorial, that same vision burst into words that would echo for generations:

"I have a dream ... "

But that dream didn't begin at the March on Washington.

It began in a humble kitchen at 2 a.m., when a trembling young pastor met God in his fear — and found vision in his surrender.

The Courage to See What Others Don't

Vision is not optimism.

It is not wishful thinking.

It is not "looking on the bright side."

Vision is **sight with substance** — the ability to see what God sees before it happens.

It's why Abraham walked in the desert, counting stars he could not yet hold.

It's why Noah built an ark before a single drop of rain fell.

It's why Moses stretched his staff over a sea that had not yet parted.

It's why young David ran toward the giant while everyone else ran from him.

Vision requires courage, not clarity.

Obedience, not certainty.

Faith, not proof.

When God gives vision, He doesn't hand you the whole blueprint.

He hands you a promise — and asks you to walk toward it.

Vision Is Born in Three Places

1. Vision is born in stillness.
   King didn't find vision in the crowd.
   He found it in a quiet kitchen with a cold cup of coffee.

You discover vision when you slow down long enough to hear God's whisper.

2. Vision is born in surrender.
   True vision begins where self-reliance ends.
   When King said, "Lord, I cannot do this alone," God showed him what He could do.
3. Vision is born in obedience.
   Vision without obedience is imagination.
   Vision with obedience becomes destiny.

When Vision Feels Impossible

God never calls us to easy things.

He calls us to eternal things.

If your vision feels too big for you, too costly, too stretching — it may be a sign it came from God. His visions always pull us beyond what our natural strength can accomplish.

King knew the danger.

He knew the cost.

But vision allowed him to walk forward anyway.

Vision sees what is **not yet**, believes what **others doubt**, and walks toward what **God promised**.

Principles for the Journey

Vision is the courage to stare into the dark and still believe dawn is on its way.

1. VISION BEGINS WHERE FEAR ENDS

Every giant of faith stood at the same crossroads — fear on one side, God's promise on the other.

"For God has not given us a spirit of fear ... "
~ 2 Timothy 1:7 (KJV)

Vision requires faith, not comfort.

2. VISION SEES PROMISE IN THE IMPOSSIBLE

When God speaks, impossibility becomes the canvas for what only Heaven can paint.

"For we walk by faith, not by sight."
~ 2 Corinthians 5:7 (KJV)

If you only believe what you can see, you will never walk in what God can do.

3. VISION REQUIRES A POSTURE OF LISTENING

God rarely shouts direction; He whispers it — and only still souls hear the map unfold.

"My sheep listen to my voice ... "
~ John 10:27 (NLT)

Hurry is the enemy of hearing.

4. VISION GROWS IN ADVERSITY

Adversity is often the wind that clears the smoke so you can finally see what God is building.

"The light shines in the darkness, and the darkness can never extinguish it."
~ John 1:5 (NLT)

Opposition often confirms calling.

5. VISION IS SUSTAINED BY PRESENCE, NOT OUTCOMES

When the future feels uncertain, God's nearness becomes the compass that keeps you moving.

"I will be with you always ... "
~ Matthew 28:20 (NLT)

You don't walk by outcomes — you walk by God's companionship.

Reflect & Apply

1. What dream or calling has God placed in your heart that feels bigger than you?

2. What fears are standing in the way of stepping toward that vision?

3. Where do you sense God whispering, "I am with you"?

4. What practical step can you take this week to move toward the future God is showing you?

5. Write a short prayer asking God to renew or sharpen your vision:

"Lord, help me see

____

____

____

____

____

____

____

____

the way You see it."

Prayer

Father, give me eyes to see what You see, a heart to believe what You speak, and courage to walk toward what seems impossible. Birth vision in me — not from my fears, but from Your presence. Help me trust Your voice and follow Your leading, even when the path is unclear. Amen.

WISDOM

LIVING WHAT YOU'VE LEARNED

> *"If you need wisdom, ask our generous God, and He will give it to you."*
> *~ James 1:5 (NLT)*

The year was 1865, and the halls of London's great hospitals echoed with a sound doctors feared more than any diagnosis: silence. Not peaceful silence — **the silence of death**.

Surgical wards reeked of infection. Patients survived operations only to die days later from gangrene, fever, or sepsis. Surgeons moved from one patient to the next without washing their hands. Blood-caked aprons were worn like badges of honor. Instruments were reused without thought. In those days, the danger wasn't the knife.

It was the surgeon.

In the midst of this grim reality, a Scottish doctor named **Joseph Lister** walked the hospital corridors with a mind full of discomfort and a heart full of conviction. He was gentle, soft-spoken, and brilliant — but what set him apart wasn't intelligence.

It was wisdom.

Lister had observed something others ignored: when wounds were kept clean, patients lived. When they weren't, they died. He began reading the latest research from a French chemist named Louis Pasteur, who claimed that invisible organisms — "germs" — were responsible for infection.

The medical world laughed.

"You want us to wash our hands because of tiny creatures we cannot see?"

"You want us to pour chemicals on wounds?"

"You want us to change the way surgery has always been done?"

But Lister wasn't chasing theories.

He was chasing truth.

One night, walking the dim wards lit only by oil lamps, he paused beside a young boy who had survived an operation but was slipping away — fever rising, breath shallow. Lister knew the boy's body was losing a battle he couldn't see.

He stepped into the cold night air outside the hospital, staring up at the cloudy London sky. "Lord," he whispered, "show me what I'm missing."

And wisdom came — not as a shout, not as a miracle, but as clarity.

Wisdom is truth applied.

Lister began experimenting with carbolic acid, cleaning instruments, sterilizing wounds, demanding his staff wash hands and wear clean clothes. He faced criticism, ridicule, and outright hostility.

But then the deaths stopped.

Patients recovered.

Infections disappeared.

Surgery changed forever.

Lister didn't just learn something — **he lived it**.

And his obedience to wisdom has saved millions upon millions of lives since.

This is wisdom the way Scripture describes it: not lofty thoughts or clever ideas, **but godly insight practiced in real life** — truth turned into action, understanding turned into obedience.

Wisdom Is Not Intelligence

The Bible never tells us to pray for intelligence. But it repeatedly commands us to seek wisdom.

- Intelligence fills your mind.
- Wisdom directs your steps.
- Intelligence builds arguments.
- Wisdom builds lives.
- Intelligence makes you smart.
- Wisdom makes you steady.

Intelligence is knowing what to say.

Wisdom is knowing when to speak ... and when to stay silent.

Intelligence may impress people.

Wisdom honors God.

Wisdom Begins With Reverence

"The fear of the Lord is the beginning of wisdom."
~ Proverbs 9:10 (KJV)

Biblical wisdom doesn't begin with knowledge.

It begins with posture — reverence toward God, humility before Him, and awareness of our need for His guidance.

It says:

"Lord, I don't want to simply know things. I want to know what You want me to do with what I know."

That is where wisdom is born.

Wisdom Grows Through Obedience

Joseph Lister wasn't the most brilliant surgeon of his day. But he was the most teachable.

He listened when others scoffed. He changed when others clung to pride. He applied truth when others defended tradition.

Wisdom grows in the soil of obedience.

You may have heard God speak to your heart —

Forgive them.

Let go.

Slow down.

Wait.

Move.

Speak.

Apologize.

Trust Me.

Wisdom is not hearing God. Wisdom is responding.

Wisdom Is Revealed in Small Choices

Some of God's greatest work in your life will happen in moments that look ordinary:

- turning away from gossip
- choosing kindness over anger
- slowing down long enough to listen
- deciding not to defend yourself
- stepping back when your emotions surge
- praying before reacting
- giving when no one sees

Wisdom isn't dramatic. It's faithful.

Wisdom Protects Your Path

> *"Wise choices will watch over you. Understanding will keep you safe."*
> *~ Proverbs 2:11 (NLT)*

Joseph Lister saved lives through wisdom that protected patients from what they could not see.

God does the same for us.

Sometimes the wisdom He gives prevents a relationship from collapsing ... a temptation from becoming a failure ... a moment of emotion from becoming a lifetime of regret.

Wisdom is not restrictive. Wisdom is protective.

Principles for the Journey

Before God opens the door, He sharpens the discernment that decides whether you should walk through it.

1. WISDOM BEGINS WITH HUMILITY

Before God can guide your steps, He first quiets the heart that thinks it already knows the way.

"God opposes the proud but gives grace to the humble."
~ James 4:6 (ESV)

Pride blocks wisdom. Humility becomes its doorway.

2. WISDOM LISTENS BEFORE IT SPEAKS

Wisdom grows in the space between impulse and response — where the soul has time to hear clearly.

"Everyone should be quick to listen, slow to speak, and slow to get angry."
~ James 1:19 (NIV)

Listening is where most wisdom begins.

3. WISDOM IS TRUTH APPLIED

Real wisdom reveals itself in the moments when conviction turns into courageous obedience.

"But anyone who hears My teaching and doesn't obey it is foolish ... "
~ Matthew 7:26 (NLT)

Hearing without doing is information. Doing what God says is wisdom.

4. WISDOM PROTECTS YOUR FUTURE

When your vision is limited, wisdom becomes the lamp that exposes what lies ahead.

"The prudent see danger and take refuge."
~ Proverbs 27:12 (NIV)

God's wisdom sees what you cannot — and guards you accordingly.

5. WISDOM IS AVAILABLE TO ANYONE WHO ASKS

God never withholds insight from the seeker; the door of understanding swings open to the one who knocks.

"If you need wisdom, ask our generous God ... "
~ James 1:5 (NLT)

You don't earn wisdom. You receive it.

Reflect & Apply

1. Where do you need God's wisdom right now — in a decision, a relationship, or a conflict?

2. Is there an area where you've been hearing God but not acting on what He has said?

3. What small daily choices could begin growing wisdom in your life?

4. How does pride show up in your reactions? Where is God calling you to humility?

5. Pray James 1:5 over your week, asking God for wisdom each morning.

Lord, give me not just knowledge, but wisdom. Teach me to listen for Your voice, to pause before reacting, and to apply what You show me. Help me walk in humility, choose obedience, and live in a way that honors You. Lead me into wisdom that protects, guides, and shapes my life. Amen.

EXCELLENCE

WHEN EXCELLENCE BECOMES WORSHIP

"Make every effort to add to your faith, virtue — (arete) — and to virtue, knowledge."
~ 2 Peter 1:5 (NLT)

"Whatever you do, work at it with all your heart, as working for the Lord, not for people."
~ Colossians 3:23 (NLT)

THE ARTISAN OF GLORY

The desert sun hung low over the Israelite camp, turning the sand to gold. Everywhere, the sounds of labor filled the air — hammers striking bronze, chisels carving wood, the rhythm of hands building something holy.

At the center of it all stood a man named **Bezalel**, son of Uri, grandson of Hur — a craftsman chosen by God.

The book of Exodus says,

> *"See, I have chosen Bezalel, and I have filled him with the Spirit of God, giving him great wisdom, ability, and expertise in all kinds of crafts."*
> *~ Exodus 31:2-3 (NLT)*

Bezalel wasn't a prophet, priest, or warrior. He wasn't a man of words or armies — he was a man of hands. And yet, he became the first person in Scripture ever described as *"filled with the Spirit of God."*

Not for preaching. Not for leading. But for creating.

As he worked, his hammer became a hymn, his chisel a prayer.

Every detail — from the golden cherubim to the embroidered veil — was shaped by divine design.

The Tabernacle rose from the wilderness dust not through thunder or miracles, but through craftsmanship.

This was "**arete**" — ἀρετή — the excellence of heaven expressed through human devotion.

It wasn't the striving of perfection, but the surrender of purpose.

Every stroke of skill, every act of precision, became worship.

When Bezalel built, he wasn't making furniture.

He was making a dwelling place for God's glory.

The Spirit of Craftsmanship

Excellence, in the eyes of God, is never about ego — it's about stewardship. When God filled Bezalel with His Spirit, He gave him not just skill, but sensitivity — the ability to listen as he worked.

Each curve of gold and each thread of blue and purple cloth carried meaning: mercy, holiness, redemption. Bezalel's excellence was guided, not guessed.

That's the difference between talent and anointing. Talent impresses; anointing inspires. Excellence that pleases God comes not from ambition, but from alignment.

God still fills people with that same Spirit today — not only preachers and singers, but teachers, builders, caregivers, artists, parents, and leaders — anyone who chooses to work with heart and humility.

Wherever the Spirit fills the work, **excellence becomes worship**.

Arete: The Excellence of the Kingdom

In the Greek language, the word arete means "excellence" or "virtue." It's the pursuit of fulfilling your purpose with diligence, integrity, and grace.

The apostle Peter wrote,

> *"By His divine power, God has given us everything we need for living a godly life .. and He has called us by His own glory and excellence (arete)."*
> *~ 2 Peter 1:3 (NLT)*

God Himself is the standard of excellence. He doesn't just call us to do our best — He calls us to reflect His best.

When you give your all, not for attention but for adoration, you are practicing arete.

When you stay faithful in small things, not for credit but for Christ, you are walking in excellence. When you care about how you serve, even when no one sees, you are building a tabernacle of glory in the ordinary.

EXCELLENCE VS. PERFECTION

Perfection seeks applause. Excellence seeks purpose.

Perfection exhausts; excellence endures. Perfection strives for control; excellence surrenders to calling.

Jesus never called His followers to perfectionism — He called them to faithfulness. Excellence, then, is not about being flawless but about being faithful to the One who called you.

When Bezalel shaped the Ark of the Covenant, he wasn't trying to impress Moses — he was responding to God's blueprint. True excellence is simply obedience performed beautifully.

THE UNSEEN WORK

There were parts of the Tabernacle no one would ever see — inner frames, sockets, pegs, and seams hidden beneath layers of gold and cloth. Yet Bezalel crafted those pieces with the same care as the visible ones.

That's how excellence works. It honors the unseen because God sees everything.

Matthew 6:4 (NLT) says,

> *"Your Father, who sees what is done in secret, will reward you."*

When your motivation is God's approval, not man's applause, your work becomes eternal. Excellence isn't about what's noticed; it's about what's known by the heart of Heaven.

Bezalel's work would one day be dismantled when Israel moved on, but his obedience still echoes through eternity.

The Sacredness of Skill

Scripture tells us Bezalel was given both **ability and understanding** — the skill to do the work and the wisdom to train others (Exodus 35:34). He didn't hoard excellence; he multiplied it.

That's another mark of arete — it inspires others to rise higher. True excellence doesn't compete; it completes. It turns labor into legacy.

When you share what God has taught you — a lesson, a craft, a kindness — you carry the spirit of Bezalel. You make the invisible glory of God visible in the work of your hands.

Principles for the Journey

Excellence is the art of letting God's Spirit shape the work of your hands and the posture of your heart.

1. EXCELLENCE BEGINS WITH BEING FILLED, NOT SKILLED

Before your hands create anything meaningful, the Spirit shapes the heart behind them.

"I have filled him with the Spirit of God, giving him great wisdom, ability, and expertise."
~ Exodus 31:3 (NLT)

Skill without the Spirit builds monuments; skill with the Spirit builds ministries.

2. EXCELLENCE IS WORSHIP IN MOTION

When the motive shifts from performance to devotion, even the mundane becomes holy ground.

"Whatever you do, do it heartily, as unto the Lord."
~ Colossians 3:23 (NLT)

Work becomes holy when the motive is to honor God.

3. EXCELLENCE IS MEASURED BY FAITHFULNESS, NOT FAME

Heaven measures success by obedience, not recognition.

"Well done, good and faithful servant."
~ Matthew 25:21 (NLT)

Heaven's applause is reserved for those who stay faithful, not flashy.

4. EXCELLENCE HONORS THE UNSEEN

What you do in silence reveals far more than what you display in the spotlight.

"Your Father who sees in secret will reward you."
~ Matthew 6:4 (NLT)

God values what no one else notices.

5. EXCELLENCE MULTIPLIES THROUGH MENTORSHIP

Excellence is never complete until it's passed from your hands into someone else's future.

"The Lord has given both him and Oholiab the ability to teach their skills to others."
~ Exodus 35:34 (NLT)

Excellence that ends with you is achievement; excellence that empowers others is legacy.

Reflect & Apply

1. What does excellence look like in the season you're in right now?

2. How can you invite the Holy Spirit into your daily work, decisions, or creativity?

3. What hidden or "unseen" tasks might God be calling you to honor with greater care?

4. Who has modeled godly excellence in your life, and how can you learn from their example?

5. What's one area of your work that could shift from routine to worship this week?

Father, thank you for filling ordinary people with Your extraordinary Spirit. Help me to see my work — no matter how small — as sacred. Let excellence flow from my devotion, not my desire for recognition. Teach me to build with reverence, to serve with diligence, and to create with compassion. May the work of my hands reflect the beauty of Your heart. And when no one else is watching, remind me that You are. In Jesus' name, Amen.

YIELDEDNESS

THE STRENGTH OF SURRENDER

"Show me the right path, O Lord; point out the road for me to follow. Lead me by Your truth and teach me."
~ Psalm 25:4-5 (NLT)

THE FOG AND THE CALL

The harbor was thick with fog that morning in 1853. Ships groaned at anchor, gulls cried overhead, and the chill of salt air clung to the ropes. A young man stood on the deck of a small vessel bound for China, his hands trembling — not from fear, but from the weight of obedience.

His name was **Hudson Taylor**. Only twenty-one, he carried little more than a few coins, a Bible, and a calling. Behind him was everything familiar — his family, his church, the comfort of home. Ahead lay a land he did not know, a language he could not yet speak, and a mission that would nearly cost him his life.

As the ship pulled away, the fog swallowed the English coast. Hudson gripped the rail and whispered,

"Lord Jesus, make me more like You."

That prayer would be tested again and again.

In China he lost his health, his comfort, and even the woman he loved. He faced betrayal, poverty, persecution, and days when the heavens seemed silent. Yet through it all, he learned that **yieldedness is not resignation — it's trust in motion**.

When no support came from England, he prayed instead of pleading.

When fellow missionaries refused to go inland, he went alone.

When custom said to keep his English clothes and ways, he yielded again — donning Chinese dress, learning their language, and living among the very people he came to love.

He stopped trying to control the work — and began to trust the Worker.

Later he would write,

"God's work done in God's way will never lack God's supply."

That was not strategy. It was surrender.

By the end of his life, Hudson Taylor's China Inland Mission had sent more than eight hundred missionaries and reached millions. But he never saw himself as a great man of faith — only a yielded one.

"I used to ask God to help me. Then I asked if I might help Him. Then I ended by asking Him to do His work through me."

He had gone to China believing he would change the world. Instead, God used China to change him.

The Posture of Yielding

To yield is not to quit — it is to **trust beyond control**.

It's loosening your grip on the wheel so that the current of God's will can carry you where effort never could.

Yieldedness is not passivity; it is participation without pretense. It's strength shaped by surrender.

When you yield, you're not dropping the oars — you're raising the sail. You stop fighting the wind and start catching it.

The sailor's secret is the believer's truth: You can't move by muscle when the Master means for you to move by wind.

The Stillness That Moves You

Yielding begins where striving ends. It's that holy pause between *"I can't"* and *"God can."*

For Hudson Taylor, that meant standing still when support failed and trusting God to fill the sails.

He discovered that waiting is not wasted time — it's worship in disguise.

Isaiah 55:8-9 (NLT) says,

> *"My thoughts are nothing like your thoughts .. And My ways are far beyond anything you could imagine."*

That is the heart of surrender: letting God write lines you wouldn't have drafted and still calling them good.

Yieldedness vs. Control

Control says, *"I must make this work."* Yieldedness says, *"Lord,* make me willing."

Control depends on outcomes; yieldedness depends on obedience. Control demands clarity; yieldedness delights in direction.

Control grabs the pen; yieldedness lets God keep writing.

You can trust a God who sees beyond the fog. When He says, *"Loosen your grip,"* it's never to make you drift — it's to move you by grace.

The Beauty of a Surrendered Life

By the time Hudson Taylor was an old man, his hair white and his hands frail, people would ask the secret of his success. He would smile softly and say, "It is not that I am a great man of faith, but that I have a great God."

The miracle of surrender is that you don't lose direction — you finally catch the wind of God. When you stop forcing outcomes, you discover that His current was carrying you all along.

Yieldedness doesn't shrink your life. It sanctifies it. It doesn't silence your calling. It tunes it to Heaven's key.

Every heart that yields becomes an instrument God can play without resistance.

Principles for the Journey

Yieldedness begins where your strength ends and God's wind takes over.

1. **YIELDEDNESS IS NOT GIVING UP; IT'S GIVING IN TO GRACE**

   When you loosen your grip, grace takes hold where effort never could.

   > *"My grace is all you need. My power works best in weakness."*
   > *~ 2 Corinthians 12:9 (NLT)*

   When you let grace steer, weakness becomes the wind that moves you forward.

2. **YIELDEDNESS ALLOWS GOD TO STEER WHERE STRIVING CANNOT**

   The heart that pauses long enough to listen becomes the heart God can lead.

   > *"Show me the right path, O Lord; point out the road for me to follow."*
   > *~ Psalm 25:4 (NLT)*

   You can't receive divine direction while rowing against it.

3. YIELDEDNESS TURNS FRAGILE VESSELS INTO INSTRUMENTS OF POWER

God does His strongest work through lives soft enough to be shaped.

"We have this treasure in jars of clay to show that the power is from God and not from us."
~ 2 Corinthians 4:7 (NLT)

God doesn't choose perfect vessels — He chooses pliable ones.

4. YIELDEDNESS CREATES SPACE FOR SUPERNATURAL PEACE

Surrender quiets the storm inside long before it calms the storm outside.

"Let the peace of Christ rule in your hearts."
~ Colossians 3:15 (NLT)

Peace doesn't come from knowing what's next, but from knowing Who leads.

5. YIELDEDNESS ENDS NOT IN LOSS BUT IN FRUITFULNESS

What feels like dying in your hands becomes multiplying in God's.

"Unless a kernel of wheat falls to the ground and dies, it remains alone; but if it dies, it bears much fruit."
~ John 12:24 (NLT)

What you lay down in trust, God raises up in testimony.

Reflect & Apply

1. Where are you fighting the current instead of catching God's wind?

2. What would surrender look like in your most uncertain circumstance right now?

3. How has God used loss or delay to steer you closer to His purpose?

4. Who models a yielded spirit that you can learn from this week?

5. In prayer today, what would it sound like to say, *"Lord, not my pace, but Yours"*?

Prayer

Father, teach me the grace of open hands. When I am tempted to control, remind me that You command the wind and waves. Show me how to raise my sail instead of rowing by fear. Fill my heart with the calm of trust and the courage of surrender. Do Your work through me, and let every release become a revelation of Your strength. In Jesus' name, Amen.

ZENI-GENESIS

NEW TRANSFORMATION, NEW BEGINNING

Zeni-Genesis: A new transformation born from a new spiritual beginning.

Zeni-Genesis brings together two movements of God's grace:

- **Genesis — the moment of new birth.**
- **Zenith — the upward path that new birth sets in motion.**

It is the holy beginning that does not leave you where you were, but lifts your life toward who God created you to become.

Simply put, Zeni-Genesis is the beginning of a transformative work — where God initiates something new in you and sets your life on an upward path toward Him.

> *"Therefore, if anyone is in Christ, he is a new creation; the old has gone, the new has come."*
> *~ 2 Corinthians 5:17 (NLT)*

The Dawn That Changed a Man

The prison gates groaned open just after dawn. Light spilled across the courtyard, catching the dust in the air and the iron in the man's chains. John Newton stepped forward slowly, squinting against the morning sun. He wasn't a prisoner this time — at least, not in body — but he still carried the weight of his past like shackles around his soul.

He had lived a life that should have ended in ruin: sailor, blasphemer, slave trader. The Atlantic had been his pulpit of sin, the slave ships his confession of guilt. Yet somewhere in the midst of a storm that nearly tore his vessel apart, he had cried out to the God he had mocked — and that night, mercy broke through the waves.

Years later, walking the quiet streets of Olney, England, Newton would still wake from dreams of the sea — the faces, the cries, the guilt. He could not undo what had been done. But he discovered something far greater: **grace does not erase history; it redeems it**.

He became a pastor. The same hands that once tied chains now turned the pages of Scripture. In that little parish, he learned what new birth truly meant — not starting over, but being *made new*.

When words failed him, he wrote songs.

And one morning, as light streamed through his study window, he penned a hymn that would echo through generations:

Amazing grace, how sweet the sound
that saved a wretch like me.
I once was lost, but now am found,
was blind, but now I see.

That was Zeni-Genesis — not a man trying to be better, but a soul reborn.

Grace had found him in the storm, but glory was found in the living — in walking each day as proof that God can bring **beauty from ashes, purpose from pain, and life from the very places we thought were dead.**

John Newton never forgot who he had been. But he learned to see himself through the eyes of the One who called him *new*.

The Miracle of Becoming

Zeni-Genesis is more than a restart — it is the holy spark at the beginning of spiritual renewal.

It is the moment God breathes life into what was dead and places your feet on an upward path toward who He created you to be.

It is not improvement.

It is not self-help.

It is resurrection.

It's grace speaking a new identity over a surrendered soul.

It's not behavior polished — it's identity reborn.

Paul wrote,

"He saved us, not because of the righteous things we had done, but because of His mercy. He washed away our sins, giving us new birth and new life through the Holy Spirit."
~ Titus 3:5 (NLT)

That is Zeni-Genesis: when mercy meets our mortality and makes something holy out of it.

The old self is not renovated; it is replaced. The guilt that once defined you becomes the canvas for glory. You don't just turn the page — you become the page God begins to write on.

FROM RUIN TO RENEWAL

John Newton's story reminds us that God's greatest miracles are not always instant; they unfold in rhythm with time. Rebirth is rarely a lightning bolt — it is a sunrise.

The darkness doesn't vanish all at once. It fades. The light doesn't demand attention — it simply rises, steady and sure.

Zeni-Genesis is that dawning grace. The morning you realize the chains that held you yesterday are now only memories — reminders of how far His mercy has carried you.

The first step in new birth is not action; it's acceptance. You stop trying to prove you've changed and simply begin living as one who has been changed.

RECEIVING ZENI-GENESIS: HOW TO BEGIN AGAIN

Grace is not earned; it's received. Zeni-Genesis — the miracle of new birth — begins when you stop striving to make life work on your own and start trusting the One who already finished the work for you.

New birth is not religion. It's relationship. It's not turning over a new leaf; it's receiving a new life. It's not about perfection; it's about a change in direction — the moment you stop running from God and start walking toward Him.

Jesus said,

> *"I tell you the truth, unless you are born again, you cannot see the Kingdom of God."*
> *~John 3:3 (NLT)*

He was not speaking of physical birth, but spiritual rebirth — the moment when the Holy Spirit awakens your heart to grace and writes a new story over your life.

The Way of New Birth

1. **Recognize your need**.

> *"For everyone has sinned; we all fall short of God's glorious standard."*
> *~ Romans 3:23 (NLT)*

Transformation begins where honesty begins.

2. **Believe in the One who saves.**

> *"But God showed His great love for us by sending Christ to die for us while we were still sinners."*
> *~ Romans 5:8 (NLT)*

Salvation is not about what you can do; it's about what Christ has already done.

3. **Receive His grace by faith.**

> *"If you openly declare that Jesus is Lord and believe in your heart that God raised Him from the dead, you will be saved."*
> *~ Romans 10:9 (NLT)*

Grace is a gift. Open your hands — and your heart — and accept it.

4. Walk in the new life He gives.

"Anyone who belongs to Christ has become a new person. The old life is gone; a new life has begun!"
~ 2 Corinthians 5:17 (NLT)

New birth is the spark; transformation is the lifelong flame.

The Evidence of New Life

How do you know you've been reborn? Not because life is easier, but because love has taken root.

A new creation bears the marks of its Creator:

- Compassion where there was once criticism.
- Patience where there was once pride.
- Gratitude where there was once guilt.

You begin to see with different eyes — to look at people not as obstacles, but as opportunities for grace.

You stop chasing worthiness and start walking in it.

John Newton carried his past like a scar, but even that became testimony. Every line of Amazing Grace is an open window into his resurrection story — proof that **rebirth is not about what you forget, but about what you've become because of it.**

Principles for the Journey

Zeni-Genesis is the birth of the life God always intended — the beginning of true transformation. The moment grace names you "new," your story shifts from who you were to who you are becoming in Christ.

1. ZENI-GENESIS IS NOT REPAIR — IT IS REBIRTH

New life doesn't rise from the fragments you fix — it rises from the grace you receive.

"Anyone who belongs to Christ has become a new person."
~ 2 Corinthians 5:17 (NLT)

Transformation begins where self-effort ends and surrender to grace begins.

2. ZENI-GENESIS REDEEMS THE PAST RATHER THAN ERASING IT

God doesn't rewrite your history — He rewrites what your history can become.

"And we know that God causes everything to work together for the good of those who love Him ..."
~ Romans 8:28 (NLT)

Your scars become the very windows where grace shines through.

3. **ZENI-GENESIS BEGINS IN A MOMENT BUT UNFOLDS OVER A LIFETIME**
   Rebirth starts instantly, but its beauty grows gradually — like light expanding across a new horizon.

   "The path of the righteous is like the first gleam of dawn, shining ever brighter."
   ~ Proverbs 4:18 (NLT)

   Salvation is instant; sanctification is a lifetime.

4. **ZENI-GENESIS PRODUCES LOVE THAT PROVES NEW LIFE IS REAL**
   New birth reveals itself not in words, but in the way your heart learns to love differently.

   "We know we have passed from death to life because we love each other."
   ~ 1 John 3:14 (NLT)

   A reborn heart loves with God's strength, not its own.

5. **ZENI-GENESIS IS NOT THE END OF YOUR STORY — IT IS GOD'S INVITATION TO A NEW ONE**
   New birth doesn't conclude your story - it opens the door to the one God always intended.

   "Behold, I am making all things new."
   ~ Revelation 21:5 (NLT)

   New birth is not a finish line; it's the opening chapter of a Spirit-transformed life.

Reflect & Apply

1. What "chains" from your past still shape how you see yourself today?

2. How has God used your broken places to bring hope to someone else?

3. In what ways is grace teaching you to live like a new creation?

4. What does "new birth" look like in this season of your life?

5. How can you share your own story of grace as a song for someone still in the storm?

____

____

____

____

____

____

____

____

New Birth is Not a Single Moment It's a Sunrise.

New birth begins in an instant, but its brilliance unfolds with time. Darkness breaks. Light spreads. And day by day, grace lifts you upward — shaping your story, redeeming your past, and carrying you toward the zenith of the life God is forming within you.

Father, I come to You today just as I am. I confess that I have tried to live life my own way, and I have fallen short. But I believe that Jesus Christ died for my sins and rose again to give me new life. I open my heart and invite You to make me new. Wash away the past, breathe Your Spirit into me, and help me live for You from this day forward. Thank You for forgiving me, for loving me, and for giving me a new beginning. In Jesus' name, Amen.

Conclusion

Becoming a Living Testimony

Transformation isn't an event — it's the rising of a new life within you. And true transformational living is found in one simple posture: a life surrendered unto the Lord.

Every principle in these pages has pointed toward this truth: when God renews your mind and reshapes your heart, your story begins to change from the inside out.

But real transformation doesn't end here. It begins the moment you carry these truths into your everyday world — into your conversations, your decisions, and the way you choose to love, forgive, and obey.

When the Holy Spirit leads your inner life, your outer life becomes a quiet, unmistakable testimony of His grace. Surrender becomes more than a word — it becomes the way you walk.

Each letter — from Attitude to Yieldedness — is a step on the path God is forming in you. A path that begins in Zeni-Genesis, the dawn of new beginnings, and rises steadily as you yield your life to His shaping hand.

This journey isn't about perfection. It's about becoming — one choice, one step, one surrendered moment at a time. Even the setbacks are part of the story God is redeeming.

So, return to these truths often. Let them anchor your heart and awaken your hope. And as you walk them out in humble surrender, may your life reflect the beauty of a grace-changed story.

You are becoming a living testimony — not because you strive harder, but because you surrender deeper.

And the journey — your journey — is just beginning.

"Anyone who belongs to Christ has become a new person. The old life is gone; a new life has begun!"
~ 2 Corinthians 5:17 (NLT)

Prayer

Lord, I surrender my life into Your hands. Let every letter of my story reveal Your heart and every step reflect Your will. Transform me daily through Your Word until my thoughts, actions, and desires are shaped by Your Spirit. Make my life a living testimony of Your grace — a surrendered story of renewal that leads others to You. Amen.

Notes

Section 1 — Scripture References

A — Attitude: The Power of Perspective

- Philippians 2:5 (NLT)
- Philippians 4:8 (NLT)
- Isaiah 26:3 (NLT)
- 1 Thessalonians 5:18 (NLT)
- Philippians 2:3 (NLT)
- 2 Corinthians 5:7 (NLT)
- Hebrews 6:19 (NLT)

B — Behavior: Walking What We Believe

- 1 John 2:6 (NLT)
- Colossians 3:17 (NLT)
- Luke 6:45 (NLT)
- John 14:15 (NLT)
- 1 John 3:18 (NLT)
- Galatians 5:22-23 (NLT)
- 2 Corinthians 5:17 (NLT)
- James 1:22 (NLT)
- Matthew 7:16 (NLT)
- Philippians 2:5 (NLT)

C — Commitment: Turning Intentions into Results

- Galatians 6:9 (NLT)
- James 1:3-4 (NLT)
- Luke 16:10 (NLT)
- Hebrews 12:1 (NLT)
- 1 Samuel 16:11-13 (NLT)
- Romans 5:3 (NLT)
- 1 Corinthians 13:13 (NLT)

D — Discipline: Training the Heart for Holiness

- Hebrews 12:10 (NLT)
- Hebrews 12:11 (NLT)
- John 8:31-32 (NLT)
- 1 Timothy 4:15 (NLT)
- Hebrews 12:6 (NLT)
- Romans 5:3-4 (NLT)
- 1 Timothy 4:7-8 (NLT)

E — Encouragement: Fuel for Endurance

- 1 Thessalonians 5:11 (NLT)
- Proverbs 12:25 (NLT)
- Isaiah 50:4 (NLT)
- 2 Corinthians 1:3-4 (NLT)
- Hebrews 10:24 (NLT)
- Proverbs 11:25 (NLT)
- Proverbs 16:24 (NLT)

F — Faith: Believing Before Seeing

- Hebrews 11:1 (NLT)
- 1 Kings 17:13-14 (NLT)
- 2 Corinthians 5:7 (NLT)
- 2 Corinthians 12:9 (NLT)
- Philippians 4:6 (NLT)
- Hebrews 10:23 (NLT)
- Proverbs 3:5 (NLT)

G — Gratitude: Shifting Our Gaze from What's Missing to What's Present

- 1 Thessalonians 5:18 (NLT)
- John 6:11 (NLT)
- Philippians 4:4 (NLT)
- Philippians 4:8 (NLT)
- Mark 8:6 (NLT)
- Colossians 3:15 (NLT)
- Psalm 100:4 (NLT)
- Romans 5:3 (NLT)

H — Hope: The Anchor of the Soul

- Hebrews 6:19 (NLT)
- Romans 8:24-25 (NLT)
- Psalm 42:11 (NLT)
- Romans 5:3 (NLT)
- Hebrews 10:23 (NLT)
- Psalm 71:5 (NLT)
- Psalm 143:5 (NLT)
- Matthew 5:16 (NLT)

I — Integrity: Who You Are When No One's Watching

- Proverbs 11:3 (NLT)
- Proverbs 10:9 (NLT)
- Psalm 101:2 (NLT)
- Psalm 139:23 (NLT)
- Proverbs 19:1 (NLT)
- 1 Peter 1:15 (NLT)

J — Joy: The Calm Delight of Trusting God

- Philippians 4:4 (NLT)
- Nehemiah 8:10 (NLT)
- Psalm 16:11 (NLT)
- 2 Corinthians 6:10 (NLT)
- 1 Thessalonians 5:18 (NLT)
- Nehemiah 8:10 (NLT)
- Psalm 118:24 (NLT)

K — Kindness: Turning Compassion Into Action

- Ephesians 4:32 (NLT)
- Proverbs 11:25 (NLT)
- Philippians 2:4 (NLT)
- 1 John 3:17 (NLT)
- 1 Corinthians 13:4 (NLT)
- Luke 6:38 (NLT)
- Titus 3:4-5 (NLT)

L — Love: The Foundation of Every Positive Mindset

- 1 Corinthians 16:14 (NLT)
- Matthew 22:37-39 (NLT)
- 1 John 4:7 (NLT)
- 1 John 4:19 (NLT)
- 1 Corinthians 13:4 (NLT)
- 1 Peter 4:8 (NLT)
- Luke 6:38 (NLT)
- 1 Corinthians 13:13 (NLT)

M — Mindfulness: Be Present, Notice God in the Moment

- Psalm 46:10 (NLT)
- Genesis 28:16 (NLT)
- John 15:4 (NLT)
- John 10:27 (NLT)
- Exodus 3:5 (NLT)

N — Nobleness: Fixing Your Thoughts on What Is Honorable

- Philippians 4:8 (NLT)
- Proverbs 11:3 (NLT)
- John 13:14 (NLT)
- Micah 6:8 (NLT)
- Galatians 6:9 (NLT)

O — Obedience: The Blessing of a Simple Yes

- 1 Samuel 15:22 (NLT)
- Philippians 2:8 (NLT)
- Hebrews 5:8 (NLT)
- John 14:15 (NLT)
- 2 Corinthians 5:7 (NLT)
- John 2:7 (NLT)
- Exodus 3:5 (NLT)
- Romans 12:1 (NLT)

P — Perseverance: The Strength to Keep Going When You Want to Quit

- Hebrews 12:1 (NLT)
- 2 Corinthians 4:8 (NLT)
- Genesis 32 (narrative reference)
- Hebrews 13:5 (NLT)
- 1 Corinthians 15:58 (NLT)
- 2 Corinthians 12:9 (NLT)
- James 1:4 (NLT)
- Isaiah 43:2 (NLT)
- Hebrews 5:8 (NLT)

Q — Quietness: Strength Is Often Found in Stillness

- Isaiah 30:15 (NLT)
- 1 Thessalonians 4:11-12 (NLT)
- 1 Kings 19:11-13 (NLT) / 1 Kings 19:12 (NLT)
- Mark 1:35 (NLT)
- Psalm 46:10 (NLT)
- Isaiah 32:17 (NLT)
- Exodus 14:14 (NLT)
- Psalm 23:2-3 (NLT)

R — Restoration: When God Rebuilds What Life Has Broken

- Isaiah 61:4 (NLT)
- Psalm 147:3 (NLT)
- Philippians 1:6 (NLT)
- Job 42:10 (NLT)
- John 20:27 (NLT)
- Galatians 6:2 (NLT)
- 2 Corinthians 12:9 (NLT)
- James 1:4 (NLT)
- Haggai 2:9 (KJV)
- Isaiah 61:4 (NLT)

S — Self-Control: Master Your Impulses — They Don't Have to Master You

- Proverbs 16:32 (NLT)
- Proverbs 25:28 (NLT)
- 1 Peter 2:23 (NLT)
- Galatians 5:22-23 (NLT)
- 2 Corinthians 3:17 (NLT)
- Romans 12:21 (NLT)
- Galatians 5:16 (NLT)
- Isaiah 40:31 (NLT)

T — Trust: Resting When You Don't Understand

- Proverbs 3:5 (NLT)
- Isaiah 26:3 (NLT)
- Psalm 37:3 (NLT)
- Psalm 46:10 (NLT)
- Hebrews 13:5 (NLT)
- Isaiah 40:31 (NLT)
- Job 13:15 (NLT)
- Hebrews 4:16 (NLT)

U — Understanding: When Clarity Comes Through Surrender

- Psalm 46:10 (NLT)
- Isaiah 40:28 (NLT)
- 2 Corinthians 5:7 (NLT)
- John 1:5 (NLT)
- James 1:5 (NLT)
- Psalm 32:8 (NLT)

V — Vision: Seeing What God Sees Before It Happens

- Proverbs 29:18 (KJV)
- Hebrews 11:1 (ESV)
- 2 Timothy 1:7 (KJV)
- 2 Corinthians 5:7 (KJV)
- John 10:27 (NLT)
- Matthew 28:20 (NLT)
- John 1:5 (NLT)

W — Wisdom: Living What You've Learned

- James 1:5 (NLT)
- Proverbs 9:10 (KJV)
- Proverbs 2:11 (NLT)
- James 4:6 (ESV)
- James 1:19 (NIV)
- Matthew 7:26 (NLT)
- Proverbs 27:12 (NIV)

X — eXcellence: When Excellence Becomes Worship

- 2 Peter 1:5 (NLT)
- Colossians 3:23 (NLT)
- Exodus 31:2-3 (NLT)
- 2 Peter 1:3 (NLT)
- Matthew 25:21 (NLT)
- Matthew 6:4 (NLT)
- Exodus 35:34 (NLT)

Y — Yieldedness: The Strength of Surrender

- Psalm 25:4-5 (NLT)
- Isaiah 55:8-9 (NLT)
- 2 Corinthians 12:9 (NLT)
- 2 Corinthians 4:7 (NLT)
- Colossians 3:15 (NLT)
- John 12:24 (NLT)

Z Zeni Genesis: New Birth, New Beginning

- 2 Corinthians 5:17 (NLT)
- Titus 3:5 (NLT)
- John 3:3 (NLT)
- Romans 3:23 (NLT)
- Romans 5:8 (NLT)
- Romans 10:9 (NLT)
- Proverbs 4:18 (NLT)
- 1 John 3:14 (NLT)
- Revelation 21:5 (NLT)
- Romans 8:28 (NLT)

Notes

Section 2 – Historical & Factual References

P — Perseverance: The Strength to Keep Going When You Want to Quit

- **Derek Redmond,** 1992 Barcelona Olympics
  Event: 400m semifinal injury & father helping him finish
  Source: IOC archives, Olympics official footage, BBC Sport reports

Q — Quietness: Strength Is Often Found in Stillness

- **Johann Heinrich Pestalozzi** (1746–1827)
  Swiss educational reformer
  Source: *Pestalozzi's Educational Writings*, Cambridge University Press; Historical biographies

R — Restoration: When God Rebuilds What Life Has Broken

- **Frauenkirche (Church of Our Lady), Dresden**
  Destroyed in 1945; rebuilt 1994–2005
  Source: Frauenkirche Dresden Foundation historical reconstruction documents

S — Self-Control: Master Your Impulses — They Don't Have to Master You

- **Nelson Mandela** (1918–2013)
  Imprisonment & leadership in South Africa
  Source: *Long Walk to Freedom* (Mandela's autobiography)

T — Trust: Resting When You Don't Understand

- **Corrie ten Boom** (1892–1983)
  Story of forgiveness & The Hiding Place
  Source: *The Hiding Place* by Corrie ten Boom

U — Understanding: When Clarity Comes Through Surrender

- **C. S. Lewis** (1898–1963)
  Used in your chapter's opening illustration or teaching
  Source: Mere Christianity (1952), *The Weight of Glory*, etc.

V — Vision: Seeing What God Sees Before It Happens

- **Martin Luther King Jr.** (1929–1968)
  1956 kitchen prayer in Montgomery
  Source: MLK's own account from *Strength to Love*; also referenced in *Stride Toward Freedom*

W — Wisdom: living What You've Learned

- **Joseph Lister — Historical account of antiseptic surgery is drawn from**:
  Lister, "On the Antiseptic Principle in the Practice of Surgery" (1867); Godlee, *Lord Lister* (1917); Sherwin, *Joseph Lister* (1957); Porter, *The Greatest Benefit to Mankind* (1997).

Y — Yieldedness: The Strength of Surrender

- **Hudson Taylor — Historical account of his missionary calling, hardships, and the founding of the China Inland Mission draws from**:
  Taylor, *Retrospect* (1894); Broomhall, *Hudson Taylor & China's Open Century* (1981–1991); Taylor & Taylor, *Hudson Taylor's Spiritual Secret* (1932); Pollock, *Hudson Taylor and Maria* (1962).

Z — Zeni-Genesis: New Birth, New Beginning

- **John Newton — Biographical material drawn from:**
  Newton, *Out of the Depths* (1764); Turner, *Amazing Grace* (2002); Dunn, F*rom Disgrace to Amazing Grace* (2013); Pollock, *Amazing Grace: John Newton's Story* (1981); *Oxford Dictionary of National Biography* (2004).

Made in the USA
Coppell, TX
20 January 2026